HAVENS OF HOPE

HAVENS OF HOPE

BIBLICAL TRUTH TO STRENGTHEN YOUR FAITH

David P. Gallagher

Foreword by Gene A. Getz

CrossLink Publishing

CrossLink Publishing
1601 Mt. Rushmore Rd, Ste 3288
Rapid City, SD 57701
www.crosslinkpublishing.com

Ordering Information:
Quantity sales. Special discounts are available on quantity purchases by corporations, associations, and others. For details, contact the "Special Sales Department" at the address above.

Havens of Hope/Gallagher —1st ed.

ISBN 978-1-63357-127-3

Library of Congress Control Number: 2018963012

First edition: 10 9 8 7 6 5 4 3 2 1

"With all the ups and downs in everyday life, who couldn't use a healthy shot of hope? Dave's easy-to-read book does just that. I've known Dave since 1981, when we both served churches around Ventura, California. He's been in the trenches. He knows what he's talking about. You will find his book inspiring, simple to read, down to earth, full of heartwarming stories, and, most of all, intricately tethered to the Word of God."

Dr. Alex F. Chisholm
Author, Pastor

"Havens of Hope is a book that points the reader to God's comfort and love. I especially enjoyed the chapter on God's faithfulness discussing Psalm 73. The practical applications were a highlight of the book. Havens of Hope is a book filled with words of encouragement."

Rev. Max Pyron
Geyer Springs FBC, Little Rock, Arkansas

"Havens of Hope sensitively addresses an issue that is central to the Christian life, and to all life: the issue of hope. We can't live without it for very long, and with it, life is an adventure of joy in the midst of adversity. This biblically based look at life gives compassionate and practical steps to help 'hope' spring anew when clouds have covered our skies. What makes this message even more inspiring is knowing the author, who writes it from personal experience."

Rev. Gary Zacharias
Pastor of Terrace Shores Church in Markesan, Wisconsin

"Dr. Dave Gallagher has written a helpful book for those under-going difficulty and for those wishing to help them. The compilation of Scriptures both throughout the book and in a compilation at the end is helpful enough—these are Scriptures that will be balm for the soul. But Dave's wise and loving exposition of these truths point us to our Savior and truly will strengthen our faith. His book is about hope. Dave brings hope through God's Word and through his pastoral care for people on a journey through despair and difficulty. I encourage you to read this book and find hope!"

Rev. Brian S. Wechsler
Executive Director, Village Missions

Dedication

This book is dedicated to my two granddaughters, Lindsey and Courtney Wood. They have given both my wife, Mary Ann, and I some beautiful pictures of hope as they have grown from infants into beautiful young ladies. I had the privilege of dedicating them to God when they were infants, and I've watched them grow into young adulthoods. As young children, they faced more than their share of challenges but always had hope and gained victory. They remind me of 2 Timothy 3:14–17 where the apostle Paul writes:

> But as for you, continue in what you have learned and have become convinced of, because you know those from whom you learned it, and how from infancy you have known the Holy Scriptures, which are able to make you wise for salvation through faith in Christ Jesus. All Scripture is God-breathed and is useful for teaching, rebuking, correcting and training in righteousness, so that the servant of God may be thoroughly equipped for every good work.

Lindsey and Courtney, you both are an inspiration to all who know you. Be faithful to God and experience the havens of hope that He offers!

> The LORD is the everlasting God, the Creator of the ends of the earth. He does not faint or grow weary; his understanding is unsearchable. He gives power to

the faint, and to him who has no might he increases strength. Even youths shall faint and be weary, and young men shall fall exhausted; but they who wait for the Lord shall renew their strength; they shall mount up with wings like eagles; they shall run and not be weary; they shall walk and not faint. Isaiah 40:28–31 ESV

Contents

Foreword

Make no mistake about it: We all need comfort and help—especially during difficult times in our lives. My good friend David Gallagher addresses this very real need. To do so, he has developed two biblical themes that cannot be separated. God is a God of hope and encouragement. But as members of the body of Christ, we are His instruments to provide this hope and encouragement to others.

Yes, during difficult periods in our lives, God the Father continues to be with us and for us! Jesus continues to walk beside us as someone who identifies perfectly and completely with our humanness. And the Holy Spirit dwells within us to give us strength to endure. But in all situations, our Lord wants to use us to comfort others with the same comfort we have received.

Enjoy this book! But more so, look for opportunities to encourage others! They are all around us.

Dr. Gene A. Getz
Professor, Pastor, Author

Acknowledgments

I am indebted to so many people:

To my amazing wife, Mary Ann, who listens to me endlessly as I share ideas and dreams, helps me keep perspective, and assists with computer issues. She is my best friend and a living example of Proverbs 31, as we have served together in ministry for over five decades. I love you, Mary Ann!

To Dr. Gene Getz, who was on the faculty at Moody Bible Institute when I was a student back in the late 1960s. He encouraged me and gave me hope to press ahead. After four decades in ministry, I was invited to serve on the Moody Alumni Board, and Dr. Getz was the Trustee representative, which gave me the opportunity to reconnect with him and cultivate a rich friendship as colleagues in ministry.

To Dr. John Hiigel, Professor of Biblical Studies at the University of Sioux Falls, who offered so many helpful suggestions as I prepared to write this book.

To Dr. Alex Chisholm, Interim Pastor of First Baptist Church in Torrance, California; Rev. Bruce Finfrock, Associate Pastor at Cherry Creek Presbyterian Church in Englewood, Colorado, Molly Wright, who edited the original proposal and all who helped by reviewing the manuscript and offering helpful suggestions.

To my son, Dr. Rod Gallagher, and my daughter, Kerri Wood; you two are the best kids any dad could ever hope for; you fill me with hope and joy.

Introduction

How great is it that God desires that we have hope, that God gives hope? Think of everything that is wrapped up in that one word: confidence, optimism, anticipation, hopefulness, and faith. Martin Luther King Jr. once said, "We must accept finite disappointments but never lose infinite hope."

Scripture tells us that Abraham was very old when God promised him a son, but he had confidence that God would fulfill that promise. "Against all hope, Abraham in hope believed" (Romans 4:18). We too can believe, have hope, and trust in God's promises (Hebrews 6:18).

This book focuses on eight "Havens of Hope" and is designed to provide strength and encouragement during particularly challenging times. In the pages that follow, you will discover the amazing wonder of God's care and faithfulness. You will feel God's healing and comfort and explore His promises, protection, and joy. The journey will conclude with an invitation for you to bask in God's love. The end of this book offers some strategies for strengthening your hope today and in the future.

Finding Hope in God's Care – Mark 4:35–41

He got up, rebuked the wind and said to the waves, "Quiet! Be still!" Then the wind died down and it was completely calm. He said to his disciples, "Why are you so afraid? Do you still have no faith?" They were terrified and asked each other, "Who is this? Even the wind and the waves obey him!" Mark 4:39–40

Picture the scene. After teaching the people all day by the sea, Jesus, now physically and emotionally tired, asks His disciples to take Him away from the crowds so he can rest.

Mark, the writer of the second gospel in the New Testament loves striking contrasts. Directly after telling the story about the confrontation with the Pharisees, which resulted in a plot against Jesus' life, Mark slows down the action with an elaborate explanation of the teachings of Jesus. Jesus, who was exhausted from being with the crowds all day, needed some time with just His disciples. This is where the drama begins. Mark 4:37 says that a furious squall came up. J.B. Phillips translates this verse as, "A violent squall of wind which drove the waves aboard the boat until it was almost swamped." The English Standard version puts it this way: "And a great windstorm arose, and the waves were breaking into the boat so that the boat was already filling."

This was a pivotal moment in the life of the disciples. A vicious storm was about to send their boat to the bottom of the sea. Fearful, they awakened Jesus. He immediately calmed the storm, which was truly a miracle to those in the boat with Him. But more importantly, He followed this action by asking His disciples two penetrating questions: "Why are you fearful? Do you still have no faith?" (v 40). At this point, they do not understand that Jesus Christ is God in flesh.

Mark makes an important distinction with this story. Even though God is all-powerful, He has not promised to protect us from all environmental catastrophes or even from deadly attacks on our lives by those who hate the message of Christ. However, He has promised never to leave us or to forsake us (Hebrews 13:5).

He has assured us that nothing can happen to us that has escaped His attention or gone beyond His loving supervision (Matthew 10:29–31). As an omniscient God, He is never asleep, even though we may at times be tempted to think He is ignoring our painful experiences.

This story of Jesus and the tempest illustrates three essential lessons for finding hope:

1. We are not alone on this journey called life, so we don't have to be afraid (Mark 4: 35–36).

Unpredictable situations occur throughout life, and no one is immune. A simple car ride can change life dramatically when there's debris in the road or someone runs a red light. Life is a series of events that we often have no control over, but we may rest in the fact that Jesus is with us. That is not to say we won't experience shock or deep frustration, but when we catch our breath and gather our wits, we may rest assured that indeed, we are not alone.

When a significant life event occurs, that's the exact time we must take a deep breath and claim God's promise that He will never leave us or forsake us. That's the time we must remember that Jesus is the storm calmer.

2. Storms often arise suddenly and can be severe (Mark 4:37).

In his book *Disappointment with God*, Christian author Philip Yancey quotes a letter that articulates the problem of unmet expectations in all its painful reality. Meg Woodson lost two children to cystic fibrosis, and her daughter's death at age twenty-three was particularly traumatic. The following words speak of her pain and doubt as she struggled to cope with what happened:

> I was sitting beside her bed a few days before her death when suddenly she began screaming. I will never forget those shrill, piercing, primal screams. It's against this background of human beings falling apart that God, who could have helped, looked down on a young woman devoted to Him, quite willing to die for Him to give Him glory, and decided to sit on His hands and let her death top the horror charts for cystic fibrosis deaths.[1]

During such tragic situations, it can be difficult to find hope. But be assured, God IS there, working in and through us. Scripture offers powerful words that reflect this truth. But the feeling that God is with us can also be found in moments of silence. There are many things that we do not understand, but it is often during life's most challenging situations that faith grips our souls and

---

1 Philip Yancey, *Disappointment with God* (Grand Rapids, MI: Zondervan, 1988), 158

leads us to trusting in God and His promises. Storms often arise suddenly and can be severe, but God is always there with us.

3. Jesus wants to be the storm calmer in our life (Mark 4:38).

At 4:00 am I received a phone call from the local hospital asking me to come to the ICU to be with a man who had been there for several days. I went to pray for the man and his wife. Over the days that followed, I was called back to the hospital numerous times because the doctors thought he was slipping away. Then, one day when my cell rang, the nurse told me it would indeed be very soon. My wife accompanied me, as I walked into the intensive care unit where the gentleman's wife was sitting by her husband's bedside, staring at the heart monitor, listening to the beeps, and watching his blood pressure numbers drop lower and lower. Any pastor or caregiver who has helped someone through a serious illness knows the deafening sound of the solid beep and the glare of the straight line on the monitor. Soon, the gentleman slipped away. In such a raw emotional moment, it's hard to imagine any good in this situation. And yet, through Scripture, prayer, and God's gentle calming and encouraging spirit, we can find peace and hope to carry on.

Clearly there are times in life when we feel that there is no hope. Whether we are sitting next to a loved one in the ICU at a hospital or are on a family trip when something goes terribly wrong, it is easy to forget that God is indeed a God of hope—no matter what the circumstances.

There is a well-known story of how the hymn, "It is Well with My Soul" was written. In 1871, the great Chicago fire destroyed all of the downtown investment properties of Haratio Spafford, a prominent American lawyer and Presbyterian church elder. Two years later, Spafford decided his family should take a vacation to Europe and sent his wife and four girls—ages eleven, nine, seven, and two—ahead while he finished up last-minute business in Chicago. Tragically, on November 22, the ship his family was aboard struck another vessel and sank within twelve minutes. Mrs. Spafford was saved, and upon arriving in England, she cabled her husband these devastating words: "Saved alone, what shall I do?" In response, Spafford sailed to England to be with her. It was while passing over the vicinity where his four daughters had perished in the ocean that he penned "It Is Well with My Soul."

Sadly, the tragedy surrounding the hymn didn't end there. Horatio and Anna returned to Chicago and gave birth to another child who died four years later of scarlet fever in 1876. Two years after that, the couple gave birth to Bertha, who would write that her parents not only suffered the pain of losing their fortune and five children but also experienced a crisis of faith as well. They wondered if their children's deaths were a punishment from God. Did He no longer love them?

In 1881, Anna gave birth to a sixth daughter, appropriately named Grace. Shortly after, the family of four moved to Jerusalem, with Horatio explaining, "Jerusalem is where my Lord lived, suffered, and conquered, and I wish to learn how to live, suffer, and especially to conquer." The family remained in Jerusalem and eventually set up a children's home.[2]

At the end of the story in Mark 4 about Jesus calming the storm, there is a fascinating and powerful surprise ending:

> He got up, rebuked the wind and said to the waves, "Quiet! Be still!" Then the wind died down and it was completely calm. He said to his disciples, "Why are you so afraid? Do you still have no faith?" They were terrified and asked each other, "Who is this? Even the wind and the waves obey him!" (vv. 39–41)

---

2 Ph.D., "Story Behind the Song: It Is Well With My Soul," *The St. Augustine Record*, October 16, 2014, http://staugustine.com/living/religion/2014-10-16/story-behind-song-it-well-my-soul.

My good friend and colleague, Rev. Bruce Finfrock, has this to say about these closing verses:

> Mark 4:39–41 offers some insights to this story that apply to our lives today. Interesting that "Jesus sent them out in the boat" undoubtedly knowing there would be a storm. Why would He do that? Why didn't He go with them? Where did He go and what did He do? "He went up on the mountain to pray." We often think about praying to God, but do we ever think that Jesus might be praying for us? But then of course, He doesn't stay up there. Instead He goes down to where they are in the midst of the storm and walks on top of the very thing they fear the most, the water. Jesus declares victory over what we fear most both by His presence, standing on top of the water, and by His proclamation, "Peace be still."[3]

As you find hope in God's care, remember:
1. Jesus is with us on our journey, so we don't have to be afraid.
2. Storms often come suddenly and can be severe.
3. Jesus wants to be the storm calmer in our lives.

As we think about finding hope in God's care, many issues come to mind, and perhaps none is more critical than finding hope in depression. Depression can leave us feeling very much alone. Depression often comes suddenly, leaving us with a great need for the comfort that only God can give.

---

3 Rev. Bruce D. Finfrock, Associate Pastor, Cherry Creek Presbyterian Church, Englewood, Colorado.

God's Care in Depression

Depression is a loss of pleasure and enjoyment of life, making you feel like there is no hope. It can also be debilitating when feelings of sadness, disappointment, and loneliness cause us to withdraw from people and activities, leaving us with feelings of hopelessness. Depression may manifest itself through various physical symptoms and discomforts, such as aches, pains, fatigue, poor digestion, and sleep disorders. The dictionary defines *depression* as "that which causes you to sink or be low in spirit; to be sad, dejected, lowering of activity and vitality, and mood swings. Depression is a withdrawal from people activities."[4]

At one time or another, almost everyone experiences depression. Unfortunately, for many, depression often lingers, resulting in a feeling of hopelessness.

Experts tell us that depression involves what's going on inside of us as well as what's happening around us. Chemical imbalances in the brain can cause depression, but so can life events, such as the death of a loved one, relationship problems, a job loss, a difficult transition, or even the birth of a baby. Specific drugs or combinations of drugs can bring on depression, as can a hormonal imbalance.

Too often, people feel that depression is just a normal part of life, so they don't seek treatment for this illness. However, depression can also be caused by poor eating habits, not getting enough rest, reaction to drugs (toxic depression), physical distress related to glands, infections of the brain and nervous system, hypoglycemia, repression of anger and anger turned inward, self-pity and self-blame, poor self image, or faulty behavior and faulty thinking. Being aware of situations that can lead to depression can help individuals find treatment if needed.

Regardless of the trigger, when experiencing depression, it's important to reach out for help—from God, from friends, from

---

4 *Webster's New Collegiate Dictionary*, s.v. "depression."

the Scriptures, or from a physician or pastor. It's also essential to remember that depression can feel overwhelming, and just like recovering from a physical ailment, it takes time to heal. The journey begins by taking tiny steps. For even making small choices increases feelings of hope, which results in a greater sense of control. Break large, overwhelming tasks into smaller manageable ones. Overall, just be patient!

Antoinette Bosco describes just how excruciating (and rewarding) overcoming depression can be:

> The trauma of depression is devastating. Friends tell you to look up and see the sun and the trees. They don't know that for you there is no sun, there are no trees. The depressed person is, like Dante's Prince of Darkness, encased in ice, in hell. When the reaction to the blows of life is depression, it is difficult to melt the ice and go on with life. But it can be done, and once you are in the light again, life takes on a beauty you couldn't have imagined before.[5]

Sometimes we lose perspective and do not stay balanced in our life, allowing depression to creep in. We may overdo good things, overeat, or push ourselves too hard. The Bible speaks about moderation in all things to help us stay balanced (Philippians 4:5-6 KJV).

God's Care on the Emotional Roller-coaster

In the Old Testament, we read about King Ahab and the prophet Elijah. In 1 Kings 18–19, Elijah is on an emotional roller-coaster. Israel has reached an all-time low in King Ahab's twenty-two-year reign. The king's marriage to Jezebel from Tyre has made things even worse. Jezebel, firmly attached to her religion,

---

5 Antoinette Bosco, *Finding Peace through Pain* (New York: Random House, 1995), 14.

has encouraged Ahab to sin against the Lord by imposing the worship of the Phoenician god Melqart ("Baal") on his people. Baal was worshipped as a weather god who could give or withhold rain.

Elijah, who had hidden at the brook Cherith for three years, emerges from his self-imposed exile to confront Ahab. In 1 Kings 17, Elijah proclaims God will send a drought if there is not repentance and a return to God. 1 Kings 18 records the stunning story of a bold Elijah meeting 450 prophets of Baal at the top of Mount Carmel. When the hundreds of prophets call to their god for fire to come down, nothing happens. Then, Elijah steps up to the altar, appeals to God, and fire descends from heaven. This is one of the most significant victories recorded in the Old Testament. And yet, immediately after winning the challenge, Elijah goes into a deep depression—to the point that he asks God to take his life.

This is because things did not turn out as Elijah had expected; for among the people, there was no revival, only anger. At the same time, because Jezebel planned to kill him, Elijah was now filled with fear.

Elijah Experienced God's Care While on an Emotional Healing Journey (1 Kings 19:5–9)

God leads Elijah to a tree out in the desert where the prophet falls asleep. Awakened by an angel, Elijah feels rested, eats, and gains strength. This passage shows a loving God giving Elijah an attitude adjustment; by rearranging his priorities, He helps Elijah refocus.

There are many lessons that we can learn from these passages, here are five:

1. Depression often follows "mountaintop" experiences.
2. Depression often comes after intense periods of stress and hyperactivity.

3. Depression often coincides with physical and emotional exhaustion.
4. Depression often follows keen disappointment.
5. Depression often results from periods of anger, if not dealt with appropriately.

It is Possible to Find Hope in God's Care When Dealing with Depression

[Note: If your depression is severe and has lasted some time, you should consult a healthcare professional. Otherwise, you may find these suggestions to be helpful.]

1. Think of something you love to do. Remember that your thoughts largely determine your emotions, and, in turn, your emotions largely determine your actions and behavior.
2. Reflect on people you love.
3. Make a list of your strengths.
4. Enjoy time with a pet.
5. Read a good book.
6. Forgive someone.
7. If able, plan a trip (long or short); get outside.
8. Stop DOING. Just be free and relax with a friend.
9. Give a small gift to someone you care about.
10. Cheer someone up.

In summary, work toward healing and hope in God's care. Make choices, even small ones, to feel less hopeless and more in control. Break large, overwhelming tasks into smaller manageable ones. Be patient!

You can take some specific positive steps to climb out of depression—especially if you're just not experiencing the joy you once knew. If that statement describes how you feel, try these ideas:

- Give praise. Rejoicing in the Lord is closely linked in Scripture with praising the Lord: "May all who are godly rejoice in the Lord and praise His holy name!" (Psalm 97:12). It's easy to become nearsighted and see only your "problems." Being with friends at church, singing praise to the Lord and engaging in good fellowship can do wonders.

- Read positive Scriptures, such as Jeremiah 15:16: "When I discovered your words, I devoured them. They are my joy and my heart's delight." Many of the psalms also lift the discouraged and depressed heart.
- Pray. Prayer is an incredible means of fighting depression and increasing joy in your life. Jesus said, "You haven't done this before. Ask, using my name, and you will receive, and you will have abundant joy" (John 16:24).
- Obey God and serve Him. Again, Jesus pointed out the benefits: "When you obey my commandments, you remain in my love, just as I obey my Father's commandments and remain in his love. I have told you these things so that you will be filled with my joy. Yes, your joy will overflow!" (John 15:10–11).

Furthermore, take care of yourself by revising your daily schedule. For instance, incorporate some practical actions, such as exercising, abdominal breathing, mental relaxation, meditation, and muscle relaxation. Take a warm bath, listen to music, or, do something for others. Seek support from family, talk about issues when necessary, and spend time with good friends.

As you grow in your healing process, try these steps for finding hope in God's care:

- Determine which situations "just happen" or are unavoidable, and which you have some control over.
- Prioritize. You don't have to finish everything on your list. Give yourself permission to spread things out over an extended period of time.
- Don't add to your list of stresses by putting unrealistic expectations on yourself or others in your life.
- Take some time out to relax.

- Talk with a trusted friend.
- Seek God and His Word.

Remember that God IS with you, and He can lift you up and carry you.

> Did you know that an eagle knows when a storm is approaching long before it breaks? The eagle will fly to some high spot and wait for the winds to come. When the storm hits, it sets its wings so that the wind will pick it up and lift it above the storm. While the storm rages below, the eagle is soaring above it. The eagle does not escape the storm. It simply uses the storm to lift it higher. It rises on the winds that bring the storm. When the storms of life come upon us—and all of us will experience them we can rise above them by setting our minds and our belief in God. The storms do not have to overcome us. We can allow God's power to lift us above them.[6]

God enables us to ride the winds of the storm that bring sickness, tragedy, failure, and disappointment into our lives. We can soar above the storm. Remember, it is not the burdens of life that weigh us down; it is how we handle them. The Bible says, "Those who hope in the Lord will renew their strength. They will soar on wings like eagles" (Isaiah 40:31)

Encouragement from Scripture:

> Therefore, since we are surrounded by such a great cloud of witnesses, let us throw off everything that hinders and the sin that so easily entangles, and let us run with perseverance the race marked out for us. Let

______

6 "The Eagle," *AllWorship*, https://www.allworship.com/allworship-inspirational-email/.

us fix our eyes on Jesus, the author, and perfecter of our faith, who for the joy set before him endured the cross, scorning its shame, and sat down at the right hand of the throne of God. Consider him who endured such opposition from sinful men, so that you will not grow weary and lose heart. (Hebrews 12:1-3)

Discussion and Reflection Questions:
1. When was a time you experienced God's care?
2. What has been your experience at being more than a conqueror as a result of God's care, power, and love?
3. Have you had a "sanctuary" experience where you were in the presence of God? Where and when? What happened?
4. Who might you listen to today? Who will God lead you to today to pray with and help share their burden?
5. What do you need to do to experience God's care?
6. How has God shown His faithfulness to you today? To your family, at your job, or with material provisions?

Finding Hope in God's Faithfulness – Psalm 73

"My flesh and my heart may fail, but God is the strength of my heart and my portion forever" Psalm 73:26.

A 1967 diving accident left a seventeen-year old paralyzed from her shoulders down. During two of years of rehabilitation, she got involved in a Bible study. Through perseverance, she learned to draw with a pencil between her teeth, and ultimately, her artwork gained national attention. Over time, she also wrote a best-selling book, had a feature-length movie made of her life and founded the national organization, Joni & Friends. Today, Joni Eareckson Tada is an advocate for people with disabilities and an internationally renowned speaker. Joni Eareckson Tada found hope in God's faithfulness.[7]

Psalm 73 begins by affirming that God is good but also emphasizes that God is faithful. God's faithfulness is a continued theme in Scripture. His promise gives us the assurance of

---

7 Joni Eareckson Tada, "Joni's Bio," *Joni & Friends,* https://www.joniandfriends.org/jonis-corner/jonis-bio/.

salvation and forgiveness, and that He will provide us strength when we face loss, sorrow, loneliness, and affliction. Along with peace and victory, we have spiritual blessings from a sovereign God. Additionally, God's faithfulness means we can reflect God's love and grace in our lives as we yield our life to Him.

The psalmist writes, "You hear, O Lord, the desire of the afflicted; you encourage them, and you listen to their cry, defending the fatherless and the oppressed, in order that man, who is of the earth, may terrify no more" (Psalm 10:17–18).

There are two certainties about God's faithfulness:
- The Bible affirms God's faithfulness.
- God is faithful to us even during times we do not feel His faithfulness.

In Lamentations, we read, "Because of the Lord's great love we are not consumed, for his compassions never fail. They are new every morning; great is your faithfulness. I say to myself, 'The Lord is my portion; therefore, wait for him'" (Lamentations 3:22–24). Psalm 36 echoes this message: "Your love, O Lord, reaches to the heavens, your faithfulness to the skies" (Psalm 36:5).

Jeremiah's condition was parallel to Judah's. His outward affliction and inward bitterness pushed him toward despair. However, his hope was sustained by recalling God's loyal covenant love and His deep compassion for His people. He claimed God's faithfulness and experienced hope through God's gracious compassion.

Psalm 73 Helps Us Experience Hope in God's Faithfulness.

First, because God created us, He understands what we are going through. "Why" questions may sometimes trip us up because there is so much in life that we do not understand. In Psalm 73:13–14, the psalmist raises the fundamental question and classic problem of the justice of God and the existence of evil, which often leads to the question, Why did this happen to me? In the Old Testament, Job struggled with this question, and yet, he remained faithful to God, knowing that God is sovereign and He understands.

Psalm 73:16 says, "When I tried to understand all this, it was oppressive to me." Sometimes we simply don't understand why we're going through a situation. Our response needs to be as the opening verse of this psalm: "Surely God is good to Israel, to those who are pure in heart" (Psalm 73:1).

Leonard Bowman wrote in his book *Hope Against Hope:*

> Trust in God's care enables a person to relax into God's hands, and gives one a sense of being one with God, at one with the only power capable of reaching through distance or delirium, the only power capable of making some good out of our helplessness and inadequacy.[8]

There are many things in this life that we do not understand, but God does. The psalmist's perspective changed when he sought God in "holy places," (v. 17) referring to the temple, and he was confronted with the holy presence of God. Then he perceived the end of the wicked and evil in this world. Psalm 73:17 says, "Till I entered the sanctuary of God; then I understood their final destiny." Sometimes we must humble ourselves before the presence of God, who is all-powerful, and simply realize that He knows and we do not.

I remember so well when I met for a weekly prayer time with an associate youth pastor on our church staff. My associate and I were facing some conflicts. I encouraged him to do certain things, and they just never seemed to get done. Every time we would meet, I would ask about the various items he needed to accomplish, and the response was always, "Not yet, but I will get

---

8 Leonard Bowman, *Hope Against Hope* (Lincoln, NE: Writers Club Press, 2001).

to them." The breakthrough came one day when he and I met in the worship center prayer room. We each prayed in generalities, but then I prayed specifically for him with words of encouragement. Then he prayed for me in very specific terms, and suddenly our differences began to fade away. That prayer time led to some tears and confession, and we both were changed men as we walked out of that prayer room.

Sometimes God uses events in life to remind us to look to Him for strength. What was obscuring the psalmist's spiritual perspective was quickly burned away by the blinding holiness of God. As Franz Delitzsch aptly summarizes: "His eyes were opened to the holy plans and ways of God and the sad end of the evil-doers was presented to him."[9]

A pastor friend received news of a terminal illness and told his congregation the following Sunday. He described his five-mile walk from the doctor's office to his home, taking time to look at the mountains, the giant trees, the river, and the big blue sky. He told them that along this journey he had spoken out loud, "I may not see you long, but I'll be alive. River, I'll be alive after you are dry. Trees, I'll be alive when you have fallen. Hope lies beyond the grave!" Death is not the end. Innumerable, indescribable, eternal glories are ahead for those who know the Lord![10]

The second way Psalm 73 helps us experience hope in God's faithfulness: God loves us even when we don't feel like He does. (He sent His Son to give us hope.)

The psalmist continues in verses 16–17 (NET), "When I tried to make sense of this, it was troubling to me. Then I entered the

---

9 Franz Delitzsch, "Commentary on Psalms" in *Commentary on the Old Testament in Ten Volumes* by C.F. Keil and F. Delitzsch, trans. James Martin (Grand Rapids, MI: Eerdmans, 1980), 318.

10 David P. Gallagher, *Aging Successfully*, (Eugene: Wipf & Stock Publishers, 2012), 95, used with permission from Wipf and Stock Publishers. www.wipfandstock.com

precincts of God's temple and understood the destiny of the wicked." Realizing God's amazing love, the psalmist writes, starting in verse 21:

> Yes, my spirit was bitter, and my insides felt a sharp pain. I was ignorant and lacked insight; I was as senseless as an animal before you. But I am continual with you; you hold my right hand. You guide me by your wise advice, and then you will lead me to a position of honor. Whom do I have in heaven but you? I desire no one but you on earth. My flesh and my heart may grow weak, but God always protects my heart and gives me stability. Yes, look! Those far from you die; you destroy everyone who is unfaithful to you. But as for me, God's presence is all I need. I have made the sovereign Lord my shelter, as I declare all the things you have done. (Psalm 73:21–28 NET)

God's holiness was impressed on the psalmist in his affliction. He realized he was always with God (vv. 23, 28), and that even after he died, God would receive him to glory (v. 24). He could reconcile his adversity—his loss of possessions and time of grief. When compared to what he already experienced in God and His love, this realization gave him hope and peace. No matter what happened to him, he knew that God loved him.[11]

When I used to lead youth camps in California, at the closing campfire we would have a sharing time around the bonfire. Campers were encouraged to stand and share what impact the week had on their life. There was some humor and some open and honest sharing, sometimes, even a request for forgiveness. At the close of those gatherings, I would always remind the campers not to rely on feelings, because feelings change. I would

---

11   Michael Rydelnik and Michael Vanlaningham, *The Moody Bible Commentary*, (Chicago: Moody Publishers, 2014), 820.

remind them that God loves us even when we don't feel like He does. Soon they would board a bus and head back home where everything was very different from the warmth of friends at camp. Soon it would be back to chores, discipline, curfews, work, school, and all that adolescent life entails. That would be time when they might feel distanced from God. I always encouraged the campers to stay in touch with solid Christian friends and be faithful in Bible study and worship. I would remind them that it is faith, not feelings, that remain. Faith in biblical truth leads us to hope!

The third way Psalm 73 helps us experience hope in God's faithfulness: God can transform and restore us. (God is a God of miracles.) God not only understands me and loves me, but He can also change me!

Psalm 73:21–23 says, "When my heart was grieved, and my spirit embittered, I was senseless and ignorant . . . Yet . . . you hold me by my right hand."

Pain and suffering do strange things to people. Bitterness often follows when grief overtakes us. When this happens, we begin to question God. We become angry and start asking "why" questions. We fail to recognize God is still there with us, offering His encouragement, peace, and love.

A little girl who was dying of leukemia. She asked the nurse for a crying doll. When the nurse asked why, she replied, "Mommy and I need to cry. Mommy won't cry in front of me, and I can't cry if Mommy doesn't. If we had a crying doll, all three of us could cry together. I think we'd feel better."[12]

Tragedy offers us an opportunity to re-evaluate our thinking. "When my heart was grieved, and my spirit embittered, I was

---

12 David P. Gallagher, *Aging Successfully*, (Eugene: Wipf & Stock Publishers, 2012), 95, used with permission from Wipf and Stock Publishers. www.wipfandstock.com

senseless and ignorant; I was a brute beast before you" (Psalm 73:21–22).

I've been with many people experiencing the ups and downs of life, and as a result, their attitude and personality have often changed. Some people can grow through their pain by keeping a positive attitude, while others continue to have great struggles. God understands. God loves you; God can change you as He guides you through your tragedy. Remember Psalm 23; I share it here in the King James language because many of us memorized this version of the psalm of comfort:

> The Lord is my shepherd; I shall not want. He maketh me to lie down in green pastures: he leadeth me beside the still waters. He restoreth my soul: he leadeth me in the paths of righteousness for his name's sake. Yea, though I walk through the valley of the shadow of death, I fear no evil: for thou art with me; thy rod and thy staff they comfort me. Thou preparest a table before me in the presence of mine enemies: thou anointest my head with oil; my cup runneth over. Surely goodness and mercy shall follow me all the days of my life: and dwell in the house of the Lord forever.

The fourth way Psalm 73 helps us experience hope in God's faithfulness: God can guide us through tough times, for He knows the beginning and the end. Psalm 73: 23–24 states, "Yet I am always with you; you hold me by my right hand. You guide me with your counsel, and afterward, you will take me into glory." God sees the big picture. We must not lose perspective.

We look around our world and see injustice, poverty, war, broken relationships, drug adiction, and so much more. As we journey through life, we experience calamity and heartache and wonder if God can guide us through the tough times we experience. But God does know what we are going through. He sent His

Son, Jesus, who experienced every heartache life had to offer. He grew weary, He had enemies who hated Him and even tried to kill Him (and ultimately did). He knew about injustice. We realize that there is much that we just do not understand, so we look to God knowing that He sees the big picture. God can guide us through tough times, for He knows the beginning and the end.

The fifth way Psalm 73 helps us experience hope in God's faithfulness: God embraces us and gives us hope. (He holds us and will keep us in His care.)

Psalm 73:23-24 says, "Yet I am always with you; you hold me by my right hand. You guide me with your counsel, and afterward, you will take me to glory." Realize that God loves you! Death is not the end. Innumerable, indescribable, eternal glories are ahead for those who know the Lord! Psalm 73:25–26 says, "Whom have I in heaven but you? And earth has nothing I desire besides you. My flesh and my heart may fail, but God is the strength of my heart and my portion forever."

Psalm 73: 27–28 reminds us that, overall, God keeps His word: "Those who are far from you will perish; you destroy all who are unfaithful to you. But as for me, it is good to be near God. I have made the Sovereign Lord my refuge; tell of all your deeds."

Consider these comforting words from selected verses in the hymn, "He Giveth More Grace" by Annie Johnson Flint:

> He giveth more grace when the burdens grow greater,
> He sendeth more strength when the labors increase;
> To added affliction, He addeth His mercy,
> To multiplied trials, His multiplied peace.
>
> When we have exhausted our store of endurance,
> When our strength has failed ere the day is half done,
> When we reach the end of our hoarded resources,
> Our Father's full giving is only begun.

His love has no limit; His grace has no measure,
His power has no boundary known unto men;
For out of His infinite riches in Jesus,
He giveth, and giveth, and giveth again!

One of the most significant challenges you might ever face is the loss of a loved one. It might begin with a medical diagnosis. From then on, you follow this person on their arduous journey as they are given the name of a specialist and then begin treatment. Endless procedures and doctor appointments consume their lives. They lose weight and grow weaker by the day. After a time, they begin to lose hope. What can you offer them at this point? Where is the hope they so desperately need? It is at this very moment that God embraces us and gives us hope. (He holds us and will keep us in His care.)

Or, the flag is carefully lifted off the casket and folded meticulously by two Marines. It is handed over to the widow, and you hear the deafening words, "On behalf of the President of the United States and a grateful nation . . ." Your heart is broken. Or, perhaps the doorbell rings. You peek out the window and see two soldiers standing stoically, side by side. You manage to open the door, but your heart has already broken before you even hear those life-changing words that your son, daughter, or husband died in battle. How will you face another day? How will your three young children understand that their brother, sister, or daddy won't be coming home to give hugs and kisses; that they will arrive in a casket?

No words can explain the emptiness of these tragic situations. Only God's strength allows you to move forward, to become a "creative survivor." Life will never be the same. But despite your loss and grief, you must press on, and with God's help, you will survive and you remember that God loves you and offers his comfort, strength and encouragement.

Encouragement from Scripture:

> Yet I am always with you; you hold me by my right hand. You guide me with your counsel, and afterward, you will take me into glory. (Psalm 73:23–24)

> I waited patiently for the Lord; he turned to me and heard my cry. (Psalm 40:1)

> "Though the mountains be shaken and the hills be removed, yet my unfailing love for you will not be shaken nor my covenant of peace be removed," says the Lord, who has compassion on you. (Isaiah 54:10).

> Carry each other's burdens, and in this way you will fulfill the law of Christ. (Galatians 6:2)

> The Maker of heaven and earth, the sea, and everything in them—the Lord, who remains faithful forever. (Psalm 146:6)

> "You will seek me and find me when you seek me with all your heart. I will be found by you," declares the Lord. (Jeremiah 29:13)

> For no matter how many promises God has made, they are "Yes" in Christ. And so through him the "Amen" is spoken by us to the glory of God. (2 Corinthians 1:20).

Psalm 73 reminds us of God's faithfulness and gives us hope:
1. God understands what we are going through. (He created me.)
2. God loves us even when we don't feel like He does. (He sent His Son to give us hope.)

3. God can transform us and restore our joy. (God is a God of miracles.)
4. God will guide us through tough times. (God knows the beginning and the end.)
5. God embraces us. (He holds us and will keep us in His care.)

Chapter 2 Discussion and Reflection Questions:
1. How do you see God's faithfulness at work in your life today?
2. When in the past has God shown His faithfulness in your life?
3. In what area of your life do you need God's unique strength today?
4. How do you feel as you realize that wherever your path goes, God is going ahead of you?
5. Looking back over your life, how has God been your faithful Deliverer?
6. What is your response to the fact that God is always with you?
7. How did God step in to give you the courage to continue?

Finding Hope in God's Healing – Psalms 42 & 43

As the deer pants for streams of water, so my soul pants for you, my God. My soul thirsts for God, for the living God. When can I go and meet with God? Psalm 42:1–2

Put your hope in God, for I will yet praise him, my Savior and my God. Psalm 43:5

"The greatest disease in the West today is not TB or leprosy; it is being unwanted, unloved, and uncared for."[13]

Are you looking for hope? Your present situation may seem unbearable, but you can find hope in God's healing power. Scripture assures us that your emotional and spiritual struggles will not last forever. God is a God of healing and renewal.

---

13 https://www.goodreads.com/work/quotes/3036286-a-simple-path

The writer of Psalms 42 and 43 was losing perspective amid the dark clouds of life. In these two psalms, the writer discusses his brokenness of despair. There seems to be a cycle: Thoughts that cause emotions, which create a mood, and the mood shapes the writer's attitude and actions. When we reflect on something humorous, we begin to smile. Likewise, if we think of a sad event and start to think negatively, we begin to feel downhearted. Negative thoughts cause emotional turmoil, even though these ideas are nearly always just distortions.

One of the sons of Korah wrote Psalms 42 and 43, which are together considered one composition in many Hebrew manuscripts. There is no doubt that the writer of these two psalms was suffering from deep depression related to what he was experiencing spiritually (42:5-6, 11; 43:5). Unlike David, who wrote Psalm 38, this spiritual depression was not caused by some specific sins in his life. Rather, this psalmist felt isolated from God because he was far from the temple in Jerusalem—many miles north, near Mount Hermon (42:6). He had been mocked and sneered at by those who provoked, "Where is your God?" (42:10). He felt forsaken by God and even unable to communicate and gain a hearing (42:1–2, 9; 43:2). But he kept on praying, seeking, and calling out to God (42:8; 43:3).[14]

The psalmist speaks of tears and asking where God is and then remembers God's presence and healing in the past (verse 4).

In the opening verse of Psalm 42, the psalmist shares his feelings about his need for spiritual strength. Then in verse 4 he speaks about remembering God in the midst of life's spiritual challenges.

> As the deer pants for streams of water, so my soul pants for you, my God. My soul thirsts for God, for the living God. When can I go and meet with God? My tears

---

14 Gene A. Getz, *Life Essentials Study Bible* (Nashville, TN: Holman Publications, 2011), 733.

have been my food day and night, while people say to me all day long, "Where is your God?" These things I remember as I pour out my soul: how I used to go to the house of God under the protection of the Mighty One with shouts of joy and praise among the festive throng. (Psalm 42:1–4)

I recently read a powerful statement by Dr. Howard Ferrin:

Human hands are poor at removing tears. If they succeed one time, other tears will come that they cannot wipe away. Only the hand that made the spirit can reach the deep sources of its sorrow or dry up the streams that issue from them. God's handkerchief is embroidered with love and tender sympathy, and it is the pierced hand of Jesus that puts it to the eyes of the weeping ones. He will dry every tear; tears of misfortune and poverty, tears of bereaved affection, tears of doubt and discouragement, tears of pain, tears of neglect, tears of yearning for what cannot be ours now. Yes, each tear will be fully wiped away by him who knows our every sorrow.[15]

Finding Hope in God's Healing. First, the psalmist discovered that God gives help when we are exhausted. Psalm 42 and 43 are one cohesive thought, worship to God's protective nature.

Psalm 42:4 says, "These things I remember as I pour out my soul . . . therefore remember." Memory can be both a terrible and beautiful thing. We may think of mistakes we've made in the past, but we may also reflect on God's forgiveness. "Grief is not a process of forgetting; it is a process of learning how to cope while remembering."Memories are an essential part of finding

---

15 Dr. Howard Ferrin quoted by David Stone, "Tears," Lakeway Baptist Church, March 22, 2009, http://www.lakewaybaptist.org/tears/.

hope after tragedy. Many feel that grief is an enemy to be avoided. Some think that they need to forget the past and move on. Not so. Grief is not our enemy; it is our friend—a friend that brings healing and hope. It is a healing ointment for the soul. It is *not* something to be feared or avoided.[16]

One of my favorite closing remarks when talking with people who have faced tragedy is, "God often washes our eyes with tears until they can behold the heavenly place where tears will be no more." God offers hope and healing!

The imagery in the opening verses of Psalm 42 is that of a deer panting for streams of water and how the soul so profoundly desires refreshment from the living God. The phrase, "As the deer pants" literally means "longs for water" . . . so, the psalmist is actually saying "my soul longs for You, O God." What a powerful image these words provide for the brokenhearted person searching for hope and healing. It illustrates the urgency of the psalmist's craving for God and the urgency of us finding healing for our broken heart.

Notice that the psalmist made this very personal by not just saying "to me," but rather, "my soul." Additionally, notice that the psalmist does not just refer to our physical needs but also our emotional and spiritual needs. He wrote, "my soul" in verses 42:1, 4, 52, and 43:6, 11. Tragedy brings with it deep feelings of loss, worry, and anxiety that wear us down physically, but our heart, soul, and emotions are also deeply hurt.

As you are experiencing grief, remember a time in the past when God was with you. I have many beautiful memories of various people and events in my past. I've saved many notes of encouragement, mementos, souvenirs, and reminders of blessings in my life.

There is an old gospel song entitled, "Precious Memories," and the words talk about how precious memories linger and flood

---

16 Doug Manning, *The Gift of Significance*, (In-Sight Books, Inc., Hereford: 1992, 31).

the soul during times of need. That song reminds us that in the stillness of the night, sacred scenes unfold. Scenes of a father or loving mother appear from years past, reflecting perhaps an old home, childhood, or other fond memory when God was there to help during a time of need. The psalmist remembered how God had helped him in the past. We must not forget how God has cared for us.

Years ago, I wrote children's Sunday school curriculum for Group Publishing. I recently received an email from Thom and Joani Schultz at Group sharing this story:

> Billy was in the fourth-grade Sunday school class. One week the lesson was about giving our plans to God. The activity was to throw paper airplanes at a target. The point was: 'Like the airplanes, life doesn't always go the way we plan, so we have to trust God.'
>
> Two years later, Billy's mom was diagnosed with brain cancer and passed away only six weeks later. At the funeral, Billy walked up to the casket and placed something in the casket. It was a paper airplane. Instead of bitterness and anger toward the God who took his mother, this boy understood that life doesn't always go the way we plan, so we have to trust God.[17]

He discovered that God offers hope in our despair.

Secondly, the psalmist reminds us that God offers hope in our despair. Psalm 42:5 says, "Why are you downcast, O my soul? Why so disturbed within me? Put your hope in God, for I will yet praise Him, my Savior and my God."

God can fill us with HOPE in despair if you just let Him. Try using a hymnal or worship chorus book to read or sing some of

---

17 Thom and Joani Schultz, email message to author.

the beautiful old hymns and gospel songs of the church or contemporary praise songs. Think of the many good things God has done for you over the years. Offer praise. The psalmist reflected on what God had done, and he gave enthusiastic praise. He discovered that God gives help when we're exhausted and that God offers hope in our despair.

Thirdly, he discovered that God delivers strength in our weakness. In Psalm 43:2, he said of God, "You are God, my stronghold." Sometimes to gain victory, we must remember what God has done and what He is now doing to help us in order to increase the strength we need to carry on. We will need to rely on God's power and His strength alone.

The prophet Isaiah offers these powerful words, "For I, the LORD your God, hold your right hand; it is I who say to you, 'Fear not, I will help you'" (Isaiah 41:10).

D.L. Moody's favorite verse was Isaiah 12:2: "I will trust and not be afraid" (NKJV). Moody used to say, "You can travel to heaven first-class or second-class. First-class is, 'I will trust and not be afraid.' Second-class is, 'When I am afraid, trust in Thee.'"[18] There is a big difference! Perhaps events are a reality check for us about what IS important in this life!

God offers Joshua these well-known words of encouragement: "Have I not commanded you? Be strong and courageous. Do not be terrified; do not be discouraged, for the Lord your God will be with you wherever you go" (Joshua 1:9).

There is an old Irish blessing that goes something like this:

> With the first light of sun, BLESS YOU
> When the long day is done, BLESS YOU

---

18 D. L. Moody quoted by Greg Laurie, "Don't Be Afraid," *A New Beginning*, https://www.oneplace.com/ministries/a-new-beginning/read/articles/dont-be-afraid-15915.html.

In your smiles and your tears, BLESS YOU
Through each day of your years, BLESS YOU[19]

It was 1636 during the Thirty Years' War. There was an unbelievable number of deaths. Godly Pastor, Rev. Martin Rinkert in one year buried 5,000 people from war—about 15 each day! He faced the worst life could offer, but he wrote this song, which we sing, often at Thanksgiving: "Now Thank We All Our God." Rev. Rinkert knew about God's light, and he shared that warmth.[20]

God's Word has the power to help us each day and give us the strength we need. The Holy Spirit indwells with power. We may not see the end right now, but we must do as the psalmist did. He claimed God as his strength.

Today you have a choice to begin your journey of finding hope in God's healing. You may choose to have a positive, healthy mindset and gain faith from the Bible and from the wisdom of those who have already taken this journey. From the outset, thank God for this book, knowing that it is intended to be a daily resource for strength, hope, and encouragement.

- You may choose to have a positive attitude.
- You may seek to discover God's purpose.
- You can experience God's healing and find hope.

Claim these two Scriptures:

> I know what it is to be in need, and I know what it is to
> have plenty. I have learned the secret of being content
> in any and every situation, whether well fed or hungry,
> whether living in plenty or want. I can do everything

---

19 "10 Irish Blessings," *Beliefnet*, http://www.beliefnet.com/inspiration/galleries/10-irish-blessings.aspx?p=9.

20 Alissa Davis, "History of the Hymn: 'Now Thank We All Our God,' " The United Methodist Church, https://www.umcdiscipleship.org/resources/history-of-hymns-now-thank-we-all-our-god.

through him who gives me strength. (Philippians
4:12–13)

"And call upon me in the day of trouble; I will deliver
you, and you will honor me." (Psalm 50:15)

If you find yourself overwhelmed by life's daily responsibilities, call on those around you for help. Don't be afraid to ask for what you need. Friends and family often want to help but don't know how. If you let them know specific ways they can help, you will be doing them, as well as yourself, a favor. Treasure your relationships. Find people with whom you can laugh and cry and share new experiences and pray with. They will help you mend your shattered life. They will reflect your best back to you, and they will plant new seeds of love for you to harvest.

We all need someone to listen to us, someone who cares. Praying is talking to God. God hears, listens, cares, and loves us. He sent Jesus to die on the cross for our sins. God responds. People today desperately need someone who will listen to them.

A friend of mine told me that he read an interesting ad in the newspaper one day that reminded him of just how desperate people can be. The announcement said that for $5.00 someone would listen to the caller for thirty minutes!

Sometimes, in desperation, we will do anything to have just one person listen to us. But God is always ready and willing to listen. Sometimes we feel like the world is crushing in on us. We live in a world filled with trouble and fear. An adage says, "Prayer changes things," but perhaps more accurately, prayer changes people. As you face this day, learn about the power of prayer.

Fourth, the psalmist discovered that God provides light in the darkness. In his dark hour, the psalmist couldn't see the light, but he knew it was there. Psalm 43:3 says: "Send forth your light and your truth, let them guide me; let them bring me to your holy mountain, to the place where you dwell." Sometimes the darkness of our circumstances consumes us to the point that we feel there is no help, hope, strength, or light. We feel like giving up, lost in darkness.

As we experience hope for God's healing, we can draw on our faith. Life now may seem unreal and wrong. You may feel cheated. You may be struggling to make sense of your tragedy, but reassure yourself that it's okay to be angry with God. A supportive faith community, pastoral leader, or spiritual counselor may be able to help you, over time, to reconcile your loss and pain with your belief in a loving, faithful God.

As we experience hope for God's healing, we need to be patient with ourselves.

Grieving has many stages, which might include shock, numbness, denial, depression, confusion, fear, anger, bitterness, guilt, regret, acceptance, and hope. These stages may come in any order, any number of times. Give yourself time to move through grief at your own pace and in your own way.

When I wake up in the morning and the sun is up and shining, I can't help but think of how good God is every day. I don't worry about the sun coming up; I know it will come up—it always does. Why? Because God is faithful. The rising sun reminded me of God's faithfulness.

Now is the time to remain open to the hurt within you and find hope. At times, you may want to suppress or avoid it with distractions and busyness, but eventually, your emotions will surface, and grief will demand your attention. Give it that attention.

The apostle Paul wrote in Philippians 4:7, "And the peace of God, which transcends all understanding, will guard your hearts and your minds in Christ Jesus."

Perspective is an essential word as we face storms in life. The Bible tells us that God IS faithful. We may not *feel* like God is faithful while we are in the midst of a storm, but our faith keeps us secure.

Remember:
1. God gives help when I'm exhausted.
2. God offers hope in my despair.
3. God delivers strength in my weakness.
4. God provides light in the darkness.

Chapter 3 Discussion and Reflection Questions:
1. What is your trust level? How close do you feel to God right now?
2. Who might you reach out to for help and support?
3. What are some of your feelings right now? List them.
4. What small step will you take today to bring some healing to your broken heart?
5. Have you been beating yourself up? Why?
6. Have you ever experienced God providing hope and comfort during a time of despair?
7. When was a time you felt there was no light at the end of the tunnel? Did God meet you there?
8. On a scale of 1 to 10, what is generally your patience level? What is your level under severe stress?

Finding Hope in God's Comfort – 2 Corinthians 1:1–7

Praise be to the God and Father of our Lord Jesus Christ, the Father of compassion and the God of all comfort, who comforts us in all our troubles, so that we can comfort those in any trouble with the comfort we ourselves receive from God. 2 Corinthians 1:3–4

The word *comfort* means "to give strength and hope." Comfort eases the grief or trouble we may be experiencing and provides consolation, relief, and solace. It is a sense of well-being and security.

The most basic form of comfort that appears in both the Old and New Testaments is encouragement, whether by words or through the presence of another in a time of need. Synonymous words and phrases are *console, help, give relief, cheer up, exhort,* and *fear not.*

In the Old Testament, *naham* is most often translated "to comfort," and in the New Testament, 2 Corinthians 1:3 tells us that God "is the God of all comfort." God is not only the creator God who consoles, but he also comes in times of calamity and gives help. He gave words of comfort specifically in Isaiah 40:1, where Isaiah exhorts, "Comfort, comfort my people, says your God."

The command of Moses to not be afraid (Exodus 14:13, Exodus 20:20) was intended to bring comfort to the people. Likewise, Isaiah intended to bring comfort as he echoed God's presence among his people: "So do not fear, for I am with you" (Isiaiah 41:10).

The second beatitude offers a blessing to those who mourn: "for they will be comforted" (Matthew 5:4). Paul's classic passages on comfort (2 Corinthians 1:3–7; 7:2–16) predominately suggest encouragement.

God is the author of comfort and comforts us in all our troubles so that we can share that comfort with others who are experiencing trouble. This is made possible through Christ and causes patient endurance to overflow to others. Paul was encouraged through the coming of Titus, who had received the comfort of the Corinthian church.

Jesus promised the disciples another Counselor (Comforter in the King James Version) who would be with them forever (John 14:26 CSB). He is the Spirit of truth; He will be sent in the name of Jesus; He will teach all things relating to what Jesus had taught them (John 14:15–27). He will be sent by Jesus after Jesus goes away. He appears in Christ's stead as mediator, intercessor, helper, and comforter: "He will convict the world concerning sin and righteousness and judgment. . . . He will guide you into all truth. He will not speak on his own authority, but whatever he hears he will speak, and he will declare to you the things that are to come" (John 16:8,13 ESV).

Walter Elwell, in *Baker's Evangelical Dictionary of Biblical Theology*, sums it all up this way:

> In both the Old and New Testament God is the author
> of comfort (Isaiah 51:12; 2 Corinthians 1:3). Christ
> is comforter, intercessor, advocate. The Holy Spirit

is the Counselor sent by Jesus to be our Comforter. The church and the Christian are to function as comforters.[21]

Our worship pastor at Palm West Community Church occasionally opens our worship service with these encouraging words:

> To all who need comfort; to all who want friendship; to those who desire acceptance; to all who want sheltering love; to those who sin and need a Savior; and whosoever will come—this church opens wide its doors, and in the name of our Lord says, WELCOME!

We can find hope in God's comfort! We find hope in God's comfort through His promises. God's promises not only bring comfort, but they give us strength, encouragement, a sense of moving ahead and . . . hope. Throughout the Bible, we find that promises are directly related to faith. Three biblical examples are Hebrews 11:6 ("And without faith it is impossible to please God, because anyone who comes to him must believe that he exists and that he rewards those who earnestly seek him"); 2 Corinthians 1:5 ("For just as we share abundantly in the sufferings of Christ, so also our comfort abounds through Christ"); and Psalm 46:1 ("God is our refuge and strength, an ever-present help in trouble").

Isaiah 26:3, is a verse that offers great comfort. "You will keep in perfect peace those whose minds are steadfast because they trust in you." Embrace God's comfort and ask God to help you face life's challenges.

The need for comfort has a "three-dimensional" aspect to it: our past, our present, and our future. We remember past sorrows

---

21 Walter A. Elwell, *Baker's Evangelical Dictionary of Biblical Theology* (Grand Rapids, Michigan: Baker Books, 1996).

and are filled with grief or regrets, and we face each day's anxieties and think about what may come next. This raises the question of guilt. We question our actions by wondering if we could we have done something differently. What if? If only . . .

Followers of Christ have comfort from God that includes true freedom from guilt. In 2 Corinthians 1:3 we are reminded that God is the "Father of compassion" and the "God of all comfort." In His mercy and love, God is eager to provide comfort to His children in all circumstances.

Whatever the trial or tragedy we may face, God knows the situation and offers hope. The fact that He is the God of all comfort teaches that all comfort ultimately comes from Him. He is our source of peace and happiness and blessing. When we bring comfort to those in trouble, it glorifies God by giving a glimpse of how He comforts those who are in distress. We are not only comforted in our troubles, but we are "more than conquerors" in them (Romans 8:37). When we turn our worries into prayers, "the God of peace will be with [us]" (Philippians 4:9).

Mrs. Charles Cowman wrote in her book, *Streams in the Desert*: "Do not run impetuously before the Lord; learn to wait His time: the minute hand, as well as the hour hand, must point the exact moment for action."[22]

I will never forget one Christmas Eve when I received a telephone call from the parents of a boy in junior high who accidentally shot himself in his right eye. Their son was in emergency surgery. I rushed to the hospital and sat with the parents through the night. Their hearts were breaking, and they began the grieving process by asking God to bring healing to not only the son but also to their broken hearts—and God did start that healing process!

---

22 Mrs. Charles E. Cowman, *Streams in the Desert* (Cowman Publications, Inc, 1925), 91.

Disappointment

Disappointment is a part of life, however, if disappointment is impacting you on a daily basis and stealing your joy, you need to remind yourself of God's powerful forgiveness and grace. What happens around us does impact our feelings and emotional stability, but God's Spirit is within us and He gives victory over circumstances that press against us. Jesus does not give our disappointments the last word. In Jesus, there is no disappointment:

> May our Lord Jesus Christ himself and God our Father, who loved us and by his grace gave us eternal encouragement and good hope, encourage your hearts and strengthen you in every good deed and word. (2 Thessalonians 2:16–17)

As we hope in God's comfort we can overcome worry and fear:

> Therefore I tell you, do not worry about your life, what you will eat or drink; or about your body, what you will wear. Is not life more important than food, and the body more important than clothes?   Look at the birds of the air; they do not sow or reap or store away in barns, and yet your heavenly Father feeds them. Are you not much more valuable than they? Who of you by worrying can add a single hour to his life?   A n d why do you worry about clothes? See how the lilies of the field grow. They do not labor or spin. (Matthew 6:25–34)

Trials and Temptations

James 1:2–4, 12 reminds us:

> Consider it pure joy, my brothers and sisters, whenever you face trials of many kinds, because you know that the testing of your faith produces perseverance. Let perseverance finish its work so that you may be mature and complete, not lacking anything. . . . Blessed is the one who perseveres under trial because, having stood the test, that person will receive the crown of life that the Lord has promised to those who love him.

These verses in the first chapter of James will help us learn to claim God's promises:

- There is an attitude I must have about my problems (v. 2).
- There is a purpose I must discover (v. 3–4).
- There are results to experience (vv. 4, 12).

Say:

- God has allowed this to come into my life, and I am under His care.
- God is in control, He is faithful, and He will keep me safe as I go through.
- God will bring me out of this in His time, and God will make the trial a blessing.

> Praise be to the God and Father of our Lord Jesus Christ, the Father of compassion and the God of all comfort, who comforts us in all our troubles so that we can comfort those in any trouble with the comfort we ourselves receive from God. For just as we share abundantly in the sufferings of Christ, so also our comfort abounds through Christ. If we are distressed, it is for your comfort and salvation; if we are comforted, it is for your comfort, which produces in you patient endurance of the same sufferings we suffer. And our hope for you is firm, because we know that just as you

share in our sufferings, so also you share in our comfort. (2 Corinthians 1:1–7)

The apostles' plea is to find hope by resting in God's comfort. In the opening greeting, instead of his typical Thanksgiving, Paul praised God for comfort; he writes about comfort in suffering; not the absence of suffering. The key verb *parakaleo* (comfort, comforts, are comforted, four times in 1:3-7) and the action noun *paraklesis* (comfort, six times) refer to the action of consoling a person. Here the consoling comes from a relationship with God and those who have experienced His consoling ministry.

The reason Paul could praise God during affliction is grounded in the character of God. God is compassionate, God is the source of all comfort, and God comforts in times of need. There is a purpose in suffering. After experiencing God's comfort, we can help others during their affliction.

Jesus came to this world to offer hope! Hope for the poor and hope for people in bondage. Hope for parents and hope for children. Hope for those trapped in addiction and broken relationships. Hope for those experiencing injustice.

There is a wonderful ministry of hope done at Palm West Community Church in Sun City West, Arizona. That ministry was birthed to give help to abused women and children. Hope Bag Ministry supports the women's shelter programs of the Phoenix Rescue Mission, the Phoenix Dream Center, and Neighborhood Ministries. The mission is to provide each woman with a Bible, in which we insert Christian literature.

In our world today, it is more important than ever that we share the Gospel message to those who are so much need of hope and needing answers to their abusive situations in life. They see no way out. Think of a child entering one of the centers. They no doubt are feeling afraid and feeling worthless and then they receive their own bag and quilt. Several times a child has asked: "You mean I can keep this?" Doesn't that break your heart to know this may be the first time in that child's life they have received a gift that is their very own? When God's children join together to share the Gospel message to abused women and children, God's light shines through their dark world and brings hope for their futures.

A Cry for Help
Claudia Smith

A baby was born in our town today,
Hid under a bridge, with no place to stay.
No doctor there to check his health,
For his mother, you see, has no wealth.
She's been abused, had to run away,
Inside her heart the world looks gray.
She makes a call to a "Safe House" for help,
As her hungry child wails out a yelp.
"Please," she cries, "We've nowhere to go,
We're alone and afraid of someone we know.
If he finds us he'll beat us and drag us back,
To a life where each day we'll endure his attack.
Please help me, my baby's growing weak,
Food, home and some love is what we seek.
Teach me to help my child and myself,
Don't push our need to the back shelf.
Show me that Jesus truly loves me,
By helping us from this abuse to be free."
Ms. Puff [23]

The wife of my associate, Ken, had leukemia. Over the years I watched their loving relationship grow deeper and deeper. But the roller-coaster of good news and bad news brought tremen-

---

23 Used with permission from Mrs Claudia Smith (Ms. Puff), active member of Palm West Community Church www.palmwestchurch.org.

dous challenges. She was in and out of the hospital and back and forth to specialists and emergency rooms. As Ken and Claire aged together and she grew weaker and weaker, the day came when she had to remain in the hospital. Their two daughters flew in to spend those final days with her. An extra bed was in the hospital room for Ken, and the girls spent some nights providing comfort too. One thing I remember so well is Ken mentioning that they could give comfort to Claire, but only God could give the genuine comfort needed during such a time. And following the loss of his dear wife, because Ken experienced comfort and healing from family, friends, and God, he was then able to help others through their grieving time.

Encouragement from Scripture

> "Fear not, for I have redeemed you; I have summoned you by name; you are mine. When you pass through the waters, I will be with you; and when you pass through the rivers, they will not sweep over you. When you walk through the fire, you will not be burned; the flames will not set you ablaze. For I am the Lord, your God, the Holy One of Israel, your Savior. . . . Since you are precious and honored in my sight, and because I love you, give people in exchange for you, and nations in exchange for your life. Do not be afraid, for I am with you." (Isaiah 43:1–5)

Here are five suggestions that may help you in finding hope during a challenging time:
1. Trust God's nearness and goodness.
2. Reach out for help.
3. Accept your feelings and allow time.
4. Take small, definite steps toward hope.
5. Be gentle and generous with yourself.

Chapter 4 Discussion and Reflection Questions:
1. What's the relationship between God's ability to comfort us and our ability to comfort others?
2. The apostle Paul found that intense pressures led him to depend on God all the more. How do you respond to pressures that seem beyond your ability to handle?
3. Whom do you know that is in need of comfort now? What do you need to do to help this person?
4. Do you need an attitude check? How can God help? How can a friend help?
5. What is tearing you apart right now? Are there any lessons in this trial?
6. When was the last time you thanked God for trials that strengthen you? Pause now and tell God how you feel.
7. How has God shown His faithfulness to you in the past?
8. What blessing could come from the trials happening in your life right now?

Finding Hope in God's Promises – Hebrews 6:13–18 & Mark 6

When God made his promise to Abraham since there was no one greater for him to swear by, he swore by himself, saying, "surely I will bless you and give you many descendants." And so after waiting patiently, Abraham received what was promised. Hebrews 6:13–15

There is an adage that states "God makes a promise; faith believes it, hope anticipates it, patience quietly awaits it." David Nicholas also said, "God's promises are like the stars; the darker the night, the brighter they shine."[24]

Here are two dozen of God's Promises at a quick glance:

- God will bless you. (Genesis 12:2)
- God will not fail you. (Joshua 1:5)
- God can heal you. (2 Kings 20:5)

---

24 David Nicholas, quoted in *The One Year Praying the Promises of God* by Cherri Fuller and Jennifer Kennedy Dean (Carol Stream, IL: Tyndale, 2012), 92.

- God is able and willing to guide, instruct, and teach you. (Psalm 32:8)
- God can deliver you. (Psalm 50:15)
- God can satisfy you. (Psalm 132:15)
- God will help you, strengthen you, and uphold you. (Isaiah 41:10)
- God will hold your hand. (Isaiah 42:6)
- God will not forget you. (Isaiah 49:15)
- God is a God of comfort, and He will comfort you. (Isaiah 66:13)
- God will forgive you. (Jeremiah 31:34)
- God will restore you. (Jeremiah 30:17)
- God is able and willing to be your God. (Ezekiel 36:28)
- God said He would put His Spirit within you. (Ezekiel 36:27)
- God can save you. (Ezekiel 36:27, 29)
- God is personal; you can love Him. (John 14:21)
- God can manifest Himself to you. (John 14:21)
- God's Son, Jesus will come again for you. (John 14:3)
- God is always eager to have a relationship with you. (Revelation 3:20)
- God will give His children a crown of life. (Revelation 2:10)

The Bible is filled with promises; whole books have been written on biblical promises. Accepting God's promises is a key to healing and peace in life. The writer of Hebrews gives some principles about God's promises. In Hebrews 6:13–18 we read the following:

> When God made his promise to Abraham, since there was no one greater for him to swear by, he swore by himself, saying, "I will surely bless you and give you many descendants." And so after waiting patiently, Abraham received what was promised. People swear

by someone greater than themselves, and the oath confirms what is said and puts an end to all argument. Because God wanted to make the unchanging nature of his purpose very clear to the heirs of what was promised, he confirmed it with an oath. God did this so that, by two unchangeable things in which it is impossible for God to lie, we who have fled to take hold of the hope set before us may be greatly encouraged.

Three certainties of God's promises: First, when God makes a promise, His promise IS certain.

> When God made his promise to Abraham, since there was no one greater for him to swear by, he swore by himself, saying, "I will surely bless you and give you many descendants." . . . Because God wanted to make the unchanging nature of his purpose very clear to the heirs of what was promised, he confirmed it with an oath. (Hebrews 6:13–14, 17)

When God made His promise to Abraham, He guaranteed this promise by adding an oath to it. God swore the oath in Genesis 22:17, and that gave absolute assurance to Abraham that the Lord would absolutely, positively multiply his children (v. 14). This oath was also intended to encourage Abraham to wait patiently for the fulfillment of the promise.

Just as God's promise were certain for Abraham, His promises are certain for us. Think of a promise that God has given to you and then take a moment to thank God for that promise. It is important that we remember that when God make a promise, that promise indeed is certain.

The second certainty we can take away from these verses in Hebrews is that when God makes a promise, the promise is on

His timeline, not ours: "And so after waiting patiently, Abraham received what was promised" (Hebrews 6:15).

After Abraham waited patiently, God blessed him. This is a powerful example for us today. The phrase, "waiting patiently" translates the participle *makrothymesas*, related to the noun patience, *makrothymias* in Hebrews 6:12. This word, common in the New Testament, refers to the ability to hold one's feelings in restraint without retaliation against others.[25]

When God makes a promise, His promise is certain, and our responsibility is to trust and wait patiently. His promise is on His timeline, not ours!

Finally, when God makes a promise, we must rest on that promise and be encouraged: "God did this so that, by two unchangeable things in which it is impossible for God to lie, we who have fled to take hold of the hope set before us may be greatly encouraged" (Hebrews 6:18).

Learning to wait and rest during that process is difficult. And being encouraged may seem nearly impossible, but faith does assure that God will accomplish His work in His time. During this waiting process, lessons are learned and our faith is strengthened.

The Gospel of Mark offers an example in this regard: Jesus miraculously feeding five thousand people. This is recorded in Mark 6:30–44. In these verses we read that the apostles gathered around Jesus and crowds began to form, growing larger and larger. Mark records that they were "like sheep without a shepherd" (v. 34). It was late in the day, and the disciples came to Jesus concerned with the size of the crowds and the lack of food. You may remember that Jesus told the disciples to give them something to eat, and clearly they were stunned, because they certainly had no food to give! Then the miracle begins. Jesus instructed the disciples to have the people sit down in groups of fifties and

---

25 Walvoord, John F. and Zuck, Roy B. *The Bible Knowledge Commentary*, Wheaton, IL: Victor Books, 1983, p 797 (Zane C. Hodges).

hundreds. He took five small loaves and two fish and looked up to heaven and gave thanks. The disciples began distributing the food, more and more until all had food to eat. The Scriptures record that there were even twelve basketfuls leftover. They all ate, and they all were satisfied. Mark records in verse 44 that the number of men who had eaten was five thousand, so think of the total number what would have included women and children! This story demonstrates how God meets the needs of people, and we and can carry that hope with us in our life today. In this story we find three important lessons of hope.

First, the people were physically hungry, and Jesus met that need. Many today are spiritually hungry. God gives His provision through His Son, Jesus Christ, and through His Word, Holy Scripture. What is your need right now? What are you hungry for? Peace? Freedom from anxiety? An untroubled heart? If you are emotionally or spiritually hungry, God will meet that need. Remember that when you are hungry, He gives His provision.

As I mentioned in the first chapter, in Mark 6:45–57 we read the well-known story of Jesus walking on the water. It begins right after Jesus fed the five thousand people. Jesus was exhausted, and He went up to a mountain to pray. Meanwhile, the disciples were out in a boat in the middle of the lake. A storm came up, and the disciples found themselves caught in the middle. Jesus saw this and came down to the shoreline and began walking on the water out to the boat. The gospel writers record that the disciples were terrified because they thought He was a ghost. And then Jesus spoke out, "Take courage! It is I. Don't be afraid" (Mark 6:50). Then He climbed into the boat, the wind calmed down, and the disciples finally recognized Him.

Second, the disciples were physically helpless. When we feel helpless, God gives us strength and encouragement.

Can you picture the helplessness of the disciples? They had experienced the miracle of Jesus feeding five thousand people. Then they climbed into a boat and were out sailing on a lake, and a huge windstorm tossed their boat around. Imagine how the disciples felt that night in the storm on the water. Then, in the midst of that turmoil, they saw a person outside of the boat seemingly walking on water, and they heard the words, "Take courage!" God is all-powerful and knows our every need. When we are helpless, He gives His presence. Now pause for a moment and thank Him for His presence. You may want to confess your doubts and ask for His forgiveness and claim His power and presence.

Finally, the disciples were physically hurting. When we are hurting, God gives His power:

> When they had crossed over, they landed at Gennesaret and anchored there. As soon as they got out of the boat, people recognized Jesus. They ran throughout that whole region and carried the sick on mats to wherever they heard he was. And wherever he went—into villages, towns or countryside—they placed the sick in the marketplaces. They begged him to let them touch even the edge of his cloak, and all who touched it were healed. (Mark 6:53–56)

These later verses in this chapter are very powerful. When we are hurting, He gives power. Think of the magnitude of that. Notice the final words in verse 56: "All who touched it were healed." When we feel helpless, Jesus gives His power. All we need to do is claim it.

There are many other places in the Bible that tell us about finding hope in God's protection. The apostle Paul also encourages us not to worry. He said that he learned to be content, no matter what his circumstances. Paul wrote in Philippians 4 and 1

Timothy 6 that nothing is gained when we worry, except to make things worse:

> I am not saying this because I am in need, for I have learned to be content whatever the circumstances. I know what it is to be in need, and I know what it is to have plenty. I have learned the secret of being content in any and every situation, whether well fed or hungry, whether living in plenty or want." (Philippians 4:11-12)

> But godliness with contentment is great gain. For we brought nothing into the world, and we can take nothing out of it. But if we have food and clothing, we will be content with that. (1 Timothy 6:6–8)

Today, with God's help let God remove all fear and worry from your day.

There are two important steps toward deliverance from fear:
- We must acknowledge our weakness.
- We must claim Jesus' power to gain strength.

> I sought the Lord, and he answered me; he delivered me from all my fears. Taste and see that the Lord is good; blessed is the man who takes refuge in him. The eyes of the Lord are on the righteous and his ears are attentive to their cry; the face of the Lord is against those who do evil, to cut off the memory of them from the earth. The righteous cry out, and the Lord hears them; he delivers them from all their troubles. The Lord is close to the brokenhearted and saves those who are crushed in spirit. Psalm 34:4, 8, 15–18

Chapter 5 Discussion and Reflection Questions:

1. What is your level of security and protection right now?
2. What does God need to do to increase your feelings of security and protection? Have you told Him about this? Why or why not?
3. Do you remember a time you felt God's warm and gentle comfort and healing? When was that and what were the circumstances?
4. When was the last time you thanked God for His healing, security, and protection? Why not pause right now and do that?
5. What promise do you need to claim from God to receive hope today?
6. What are the specific battles going on in your life today? What is your response to God?
7. What is the relationship between crisis and faith in your life?
8. In what specific areas of your life do you need to take courage, not be afraid, and claim God's promises?
9. How has He delivered you from your fears?
10. Describe the last time you were crushed in spirit and you felt the Lord close to you.

Finding Hope in God's Protection – Psalm 91

"Because he loves me," says the Lord, "I will rescue him; I will protect him, for he acknowledges my name. He will call on me, and I will answer him; I will be with him in trouble, I will deliver him and honor him. With long life I will satisfy him and show him my salvation."
Psalm 91:14–16

Many years ago, my wife and I were visiting her parents in Wisconsin. My wife's brother was there for several days, and we had a good family visit. Her grandparents founded a mission working with Native Americans, and my wife's father took over the mission when her grandfather was unable to continue leading it.

We thought it might be nice to go on a local campout, just her brother and me. We packed camping gear and headed off to a remote spot to spend the night under the stars. In the middle of the night, when we were sound asleep, we heard loud voices. When we got up to investigate, we met a group of Native Americans who had been drinking. They angrily asked what we were doing on *their* property. When we tried to explain, they only became more hostile and began saying that they were going to kill us both! My mind went to Psalm 91:14–15 and the words, "I will rescue him, I will protect him, for he acknowledges my name. He will call on me, and I will answer him; I will be with him in trouble." Then my brother-in-law made a statement that stopped everything. He mentioned that his dad was Rev. Avery Wetzig, and nothing else needed to be said.

Immediately the group began to apologize and ask for forgiveness. It wasn't my name or my brother-in-law's name that made the difference. It was his father's name, the director of the Midwest Indian Mission, that made the difference. They quietly left, expressing thanks to the Mission and for Rev. Avery Wetzig. I was thinking of our heavenly Father and His name.

Our hope is not found in earthly goods or circumstances. Our hope is found in God. As we turn to God, we learn to be open to God's safety and blessing. As we learn and grow through challenging times, we may become instruments of God and His grace and find ways to help others.

We all need hope in so many different avenues of life. The poor hope for the means to meet their basic needs. Those in bondage hope for freedom. The unemployed hope to find work, and parents hope for healthy children. We all hope for friends and healthy relationships. If a relationship is broken, we hope for forgiveness and reconciliation. We hope the crippling bondage of addiction will release its hold over those we love. In a world of injustice, we hope justice will prevail.

When a loved one passes away, our hope can shatter. I remember a dear elderly woman who had a standing appointment with me on the anniversary of the loss of her husband. I tried to help her move on with her life without success. It is important that we remember that the source of our security is found in the Lord.

In Psalm 91 we read words of hope:

Whoever dwells in the shelter of the Most High will rest in the shadow of the Almighty. I will say of the Lord, "He is my refuge and my fortress, my God, in whom I trust." Surely he will save you from the fowler's snare and from the deadly pestilence. He will cover you with his feathers, and under his wings you will find refuge; his faithfulness will be your shield and rampart. You will not fear the terror of night, nor the arrow that flies by day, nor the pestilence that stalks in the darkness, nor the plague that destroys at midday. A thousand may fall at your side, ten thousand at your right hand, but it will not come near you. You will only observe with your eyes and see the punishment of the wicked. If you say, "The Lord is my refuge," and you make the Most High your dwelling, no harm will overtake you, no disaster will come near your tent. For he will command his angels concerning you to guard you in all your ways; they will lift you up in their hands, so that you will not strike your foot against a stone. You will tread on the lion and the cobra; you will trample the great lion and the serpent. "Because he loves me," says the Lord, "I will rescue him; I will protect him, for he acknowledges my name. He will call on me, and I will answer him; I will be with him in trouble, I will deliver him and honor him. With long life I will satisfy him and show him my salvation."

Think of some of the lessons given in these verses. First, we can have hope because God's protection gives us rest (v. 1). Psalm 91 is about the source and security of believers. The first two verses remind us that the source of our security is found in the Lord:

> Whoever dwells in the shelter of the Most High will rest in the shadow of the Almighty. I will say of the Lord, "He is my refuge and my fortress, my God, in whom I trust." (Psalm 91:1–2)

One of my favorite hymns is, "This Is My Father's World." This hymn was written by Maltie D. Babcock in 1901, and the fourth verse reminds us of the bright future and hope that we have by God's grace:

> This is my Father's world:
> Oh, let me ne'er forget,
> That though the wrong seems oft so strong,
> God is the ruler yet.

> This is my Father's world,
> The battle is not done:
> Jesus who died shall be satisfied,
> And earth and Heav'n be one."[26]

Second, we can have hope because God is our shield (v. 3–4):

> Surely he will save you from the fowler's snare and the deadly pestilence. He will cover you with his feathers, and under his wings, you will find refuge; his faithfulness will be your shield and rampart. (Psalm 92:3–4)

When you are searching for hope, turn to God. When you experience a life challenge, remember that you are vulnerable and fragile. That is not the time to make major decisions; it's the time

---

26 "This Is My Father's World," lyrics by Maltie D. Babcock, https://library.timelesstruths.org/music/This_Is_My_Fathers_World/

to draw near to God and faithful friends for encouragement and support. I strongly encourage you to get involved in a grief support group as soon as you feel comfortable doing so. The protection God will give comes from His faithfulness. Remember that there are stages of the grieving process. Some people do move from one stage to another, but others do not, and the phases they experience may feel mixed up and confused. We often hear that someone suffering loss experiences shock and then moves on perhaps to denial, resentment, anger, and maybe then acceptance, and readjustment, however, these often become blended.[27] For a discussion about the stages of grief, see any of Elisabeth Kubler Ross's books, like *Death: The Final Stage of Growth*, *On Death and Dying*, or *Living with Death and Dying*. These works are available in various editions and reprints.

Third, we can have hope because God's protection is unceasing (v. 5). In verses 5–6, the psalmist gives some specific examples of times of loss and reminds us that God is on watch, protecting us with His gentle and warm love every moment of every day and night. This psalm encourages us to find refuge in God during times of disaster.

> You will not fear the terror of night, nor the arrow that flies by day, nor the pestilence that stalks in the darkness, nor the plague that destroys at midday. (Psalm 92:5–6)

There is a beautiful worship song written by Rich Mullins that says, "Our God is an Awesome God" that may be sung after reading these verses![28]

---

27   Michael Rydelnik and Michael Vanlaningham, *The Moody Bible Commentary*, (Chicago: Moody Publishers, 2014), 834.

28   "Our God Is an Awesome God," lyrics by Rich Mullins, https://genius.com/Rich-mullins-awesome-god-lyrics

Fourth, we can have hope because we have certainty that God is our refuge (v. 9).

The parallel numeric poetic construction of "a thousand" and "ten thousand" expresses extreme security against anything and anyone. Notice the ending phrase of verse 7 that "it [danger] will not come near you." What security and protection we have in God! We are reminded again in verse 10 that no harm will overtake us, no disaster will come that we cannot bear; God is with us.

> A thousand may fall at your side, ten thousand at your right hand, but it will not come near you. You will only observe with your eyes and see the punishment of the wicked. If you say, "The LORD is my refuge," and you make the Most High your dwelling, no harm will overtake you, no disaster will come near your tent. For he will command his angels concerning you to guard you in all your ways; they will lift you up in their hands, so that you will not strike your foot against a stone. (Psalm 92:7–12)

There are many hurting hearts today. Whenever hurt or pain comes into our life, there is a tendency to pull back. The very thing we need to do is what we do not do. We need God, and we need other people for strength and encouragement. The psalmist wrote about that. Read through Psalm 91 to gain comfort for a hurting heart.

We Have a Bright Future

With our world filled with violence, it is difficult to think that there is a bright future—but there is! Remember that God is still in control. We do have a bright future because of our Father's love for us. It's easy to lose perspective and dwell on the negative when we watch the news on television and read the newspaper reporting the horrible events taking place. But we must maintain perspective and remember that we have a bright future and that God is sovereign.

Being Released from Worry and Anxiety

It's so easy to carry around a bag of worry. We allow ourselves to "wallow in self-pity." Peter reminds us that we are to cast off our anxiety, and he gives us the reason we should do so as well: because God cares for us (1 Peter 5:7). Psalm 55:22 instructs the same: "Cast your cares on the Lord and he will sustain you; he will never let the righteous fall."

In Matthew 5:4 Jesus gave a special blessing to those who are hurting! "Blessed are those who mourn, for they will be comforted."

"Mourning" affects your relationship with God and brings you together in forgiveness and humility.

"Mourning" affects your personally and it affects your attitudes and actions.

"Mourning" affects your relationship with others around you.

Once when I was with a patient before surgery, I intended to read some Scripture and offer a word of encouragement and prayer for God's guidance and peace. After I read and said a few words of encouragement, I was just about to pray when a nurse came to the man's bed. She checked his chart, made sure that everything was in order, and told me that he would be going to surgery very shortly. The doctor and the nurse had said earlier that attitude was critical before surgery, but the man had said over and over to his wife that he was sure he would not come out of the surgery alive. That nurse had leaned over the bed, looked right into the man's eyes, and said very sternly, "No more of that negative talk now. I've been a nurse for over fifteen years and know that the attitude you have going into surgery greatly impacts the results and recovery." Attitude! Perspective! Whatever your situation, why not choose to have a positive attitude? That patient came through surgery just fine.

Chapter 6 Discussion and Reflection Questions:
1. Do you truly believe that Jesus is a joy-giver? If so, have you thanked Him for His joy? If not, why?
2. When was a recent time you experienced God's protection?
3. How did God use others to help you during a time of crisis?
4. What does it mean to make God your refuge?
5. As you think about any potential harm that could come in your life, do you truly believe that angels will be guarding you? Why or why not?

Finding Hope in God's Joy – Psalm 100 & Philippians

Shout for joy to the Lord, all the earth. Worship the Lord with gladness; come before him with joyful songs. Know that the Lord is God. It is he who made us, and we are his; we are his people, the sheep of his pasture. Enter his gates with thanksgiving and his courts with praise; give thanks to him and praise his name. For the Lord is good and his love endures forever; his faithfulness continues through all generations. Psalm 100

My wife is from a very large, close-knit family. She is one of six children and has two brothers and three sisters. The two brothers are pastors, just like her dad and her grandfather. All her siblings are active in local churches, and every few years the entire family gets together for a family reunion. I can think of no better example of joy than when her family all gathers together. Probably the most noticeable characteristic of these get-togethers is how much the siblings laugh when they are together. In fact, once they gather around a table to play games, you can expect loud ruckus and hilarious laughter for hours. They always experience tremendous joy in one another's company.

Joy has amazing healing power. Proverbs 17:22 so aptly reminds us that a cheerful heart is good medicine.

The Old Testament book of Psalms offers a range of human responses to God and His word. The 150 Psalms contained in the Bible formed a hymnbook for the Israelites. Most of the various psalms were used in Israel's worship over the centuries. Some psalms were connected to certain feasts (Psalm 130 for Yom Kippur; Psalm 135 for Passover). Others were connected to the Sabbath, and still others to confession or praise.

When I was in high school, the church our family attended had a wonderful choir. They would almost always come in with an opening anthem of praise to God. I remember so well many Sundays hearing a majestic, rousing chorus of praise, "Enter into His gates with thanksgiving, and into His courts with praise, be thankful unto Him, be thankful unto Him and bless His name, and bless His name, Amen." As the choir offered this call to worship, the pastor would come out and walk to the pulpit. When the choir finished that powerful call to worship, the pastor led an invocation, and we'd begin singing hymns and choruses to exalt the name of Christ. It is amazing how various aspects of worship impact lives.

Psalm 100 reminds us and encourages us to give grateful praise to God. The first verse invites us to shout joyfully to the Lord. Psalm 100 was addressed to the people of Israel but provides a wonderful reminder of how gathering together with other followers of Christ to worship Him can be a powerful experience. As we worship together with gladness and joyful songs, we reflect on the Lord's goodness and affirm that all that we are and all that have is from a loving, caring, heavenly Father. As we hear the Scriptures read, fellowship with believers, and give God a portion of what He has given to us, we gain a new, fresh reason to find hope in God's joy.

The Bible is a book of joy. In John 10:10, Jesus makes a profound statement about fulfillment in life: "I am come that we might have life and have it more abundantly." The word *abundantly* means "plentifully, fully, sufficiently, and adequately." Not many people today are enjoying that type of life. And in John 15:11 we read, "I have told you this so that my joy may be in you and that your joy may be complete."

The book of Philippians is one of the most joyful books in the entire Bible. Here are just a few encouraging words found in Philippians:

> In all my prayers for all of you, I always pray with joy.
> (Philippians 1:4)

> Convinced of this, I know that remain, and continue
> with all of you for your progress and joy in the faith.
> (Philippians 1:25)

> Then make my joy complete by being like-minded,
> having the same love, being one in spirit and of one
> mind. (Philippians 2:2)

> So then, welcome him in the Lord with great joy, and
> honor people like him. (Philippians 2:29)

> Therefore, my brothers and sisters, you whom I love
> and long for, my joy and crown, stand firm in the Lord
> in this way, dear friends! (Philippians 4:1)

If you are seeking joy, try reading through the book of Philippians.

John Powell wrote an excellent book entitled *Happiness Is an Inside Job*. I agree with his message that our world may fall apart, but we can still experience joy.

Happiness centers around things. Joy is found only in a right relationship with God. Joy is found in having a relationship with God through His Son, Jesus Christ. As events take place in our lives we have a choice. We learn lessons and grow, or we react and rebel often making everyone around us miserable.[29]

It is reported that Evansburg, a small town in Canada, became known as, "Home of the town of the Grouch." Reportedly, the tradition began in 1961, when local artist John Lauer was commissioned to make a new welcome sign for the community. To add some humor, he added to the sign, "603 people, 29 dogs, 41 cats, and one grouch."

Unfortunately, in most companies of people, there is one grouch—one person who complains constantly or who always sees the dark side of things. In churches, too, there seems to always be one grouch around.

We do have a choice. We recently purchased a new king-sized bed with a state-of-the-art adjustable base. You just push a button to lift your head or feet or another button to initiate relaxing vibrations. It was guaranteed for ten years! When it was delivered and set up, it was a joy to lie down in absolute comfort. My wife and I were thrilled with our new purchase . . . until a few days later when I raised my half of the bed up and found that it wouldn't go back down. We worked at it without results. We called the warranty number, and they assured us that it could be easily fixed. As we listened on speakerphone to the instructions, we calmly crawled under the bed and pushed this button and that button, watching computer lights come on and off with no results. We were leaving for a weeklong trip back to the Midwest and needed this expensive new bed fixed. We were told that a new electronic

---

29 John Powell, *Happiness Is an Inside Job* (Allen, TX: RCL, 1999).

control would be shipped to us at no cost. Unfortunately, that meant that my side of the bed became the floor!

Long story short, my patience began to waver. My attitude was moving from praise and rejoicing to . . . grumbling. I was allowing myself to get sucked up into negative thinking, and I needed to remind myself that this was not the end of the world. I needed to be reminded that my joy did not depend on an expensive mattress; I had a choice.

Charles Swindoll wrote:

> The longer I live, the more I realize the impact of attitude on life. Attitude, to me, is more important than facts. It is more important than the past, than education, than money, than circumstances, than failures, than successes, than what other people think or say or do. It is more important than appearance, giftedness, or skill. It will make or break a company, a church, a home. The remarkable thing is that we have a choice every day regarding the attitude we will have for that day. We cannot change the inevitable. The only thing we can do is play on the one string we have, and that is our attitude . . . I am convinced that life is 10% what happens to me and 90% how I react to it. And so, it is with you . . . we are in charge of our Attitudes.[30]

When we lived in Santa Monica, California, and our two adult children had moved away, we were alone. My wife and I would go to Santa Monica Civic Auditorium on Thanksgiving Day and help feed thousands of homeless people. We must never take for granted the blessings we have.

I have learned that life is very fragile and that we do not have tomorrow. Also, while living in Santa Monica, our church had a team of volunteers who would make three hundred brown bag

---

30 Charles Swindoll, "Attitude," https://www.bigeye.com/attitude.htm.

lunches each day. Every morning homeless men and women would come to the church early, line up orderly, and receive a brown bag meal. As our volunteers handed each person a lunch for the day, they would say these words: "In the name of Jesus and His love, I give you this food." Those homeless folks were filled with joy and were very grateful for the blessing given them. And I was filled with joy as I was able to make just a small token of God's love tangible.

Real joy says, "Fear not!" True joy believes that God does bring us "good tidings." Joy does not entail ignoring hurt, pain, or loss. It believes that God does bring us good tidings of great joy, acknowledges that happiness is wrapped up in things, and that joy is found only in God's peace. It is admitting that God is on the throne. God cares, God is sovereign, God loves us. God will take care of us no matter what. Joy has a positive attitude in the midst of the storm. Real joy acknowledges that God can give comfort to everyone. Joy is found only in Jesus who said, "Come to me, all you who are weary and burdened, and I will give you rest" (Matthew 11:28). Jesus is the great "joy-giver."

Psalm 42:4–6 says:

> These things I remember as I pour out my soul: how I used to go with the multitude, leading the procession to the house of God, with shouts of joy and thanksgiving among the festive throng. Why are you downcast, O my soul? Why so disturbed within me? Put your hope in God, for yet praise him, my Savior and my God.

In Matthew 2:10 (NIV) we read, "When they saw the star, they were overjoyed." That same verse in the King James Version reads, "When they saw the star, they rejoiced with exceeding great joy."

In Luke 2:10 (NIV) we read, "But the angel said to them, 'Do not be afraid. I bring you good news of great joy that will be for all the people.'" In the King James Version, it is recorded as, "And the angel said unto them, Fear not: for, behold, I bring you good tidings of great joy, which shall be to all people."

It is a beautiful thought to realize that God's Son, Jesus, is in heaven right now interceding for us and our needs. When I pray, Jesus intercedes. When I present a request in prayer, Jesus presents that to God the Father. Paul writes about that wonderful process in Romans 8. In the same chapter, Paul also gives us great encouragement, reminding us that nothing will separate us from God's love.

All through Scripture we find people praising the Lord in all sorts of situations. For instance, when Nehemiah faced horrendous life challenges, he declared, "For the joy of the Lord is your strength" (Nehemiah 8:10).

The psalmist wrote, "Praise be to the Lord, to God our Savior, who daily bears our burdens. Selah" (Psalm 68:19). And in Psalm 100, the psalmist bursts forth with joy and praise when he writes, "Praise the Lord!" *Praise* is a wonderful word. Praise opens us up and gives us release. Praise exalts the name of our Lord and pleases God. Praise is good medicine, as is laughter. It is important to give thanks. It is important to lift praise up to the Lord. The writer of the book of Hebrews declares, "Through Jesus, therefore, let us continually offer to God a sacrifice of praise— the fruit of lips that confess his name" (Hebrews 13:15).

Gifts are lovely, especially personal gifts. When God sent His Son Jesus to this world, it was an incredibly intimate act. Jesus came for you! He came that you might live. Perhaps the best-known verse in the entire Bible declares:

> For God so loved the world that he gave his one and only Son, that whoever believes in him shall not perish but have eternal life. For God did not send his Son into the world to condemn the world, but to save the world through him. Whoever believes in him is not

condemned, but whoever does not believe stands condemned already because he has not believed in the name of God's one and only Son." (John 3:16–18)

And in 1 John 4:9 we read, "This is how God showed his love among us: He sent his one and only Son into the world that we might live through him."

It is time to become stronger and experience hope and victory. You have read in these pages about scores of practical steps that you may take. I encourage you to go back and make a note of some of the suggestions that you can incorporate into your life. Expect God to do a work in your life; expect a miracle. We serve a mighty God who loves you and wants you to experience comfort and healing. Use what you have read as a stepping stone—a bridge—to cross over from despair to joy.

No matter what your situation, there is always hope.

In May of 2016, my wife's mother was approaching her closing days on this earth and preparing for her eternal home in heaven. There were times that she felt that she hadn't impacted the lives of others. In the last week of her life, many people from the small community in Wisconsin, came by to see her. They told her how much she impacted their lives. That brought great joy and comfort in her final days. Her immediate response was a desire to share that joy with others. She began going up and down the hall of that care center to visit and encourage other patients. She read Scripture to them and prayed for each person she shared with, bringing them great hope and joy. God gave her great peace in her final hours, and she slipped into eternity experiencing God's peace and joy.

What challenges are you facing right now? What is your attitude about that challenge? Are you angry or bitter? Or can you move past those feelings to let God change your heart and give you hope and joy? Can you reach out to someone, even as you face your challenge and offer hope and joy to someone else?

Chapter 7 Discussion and Reflection Questions:

1. Is your expression of joy too limited?
2. What is your joy level today?
3. When was the last time you talked to God about this?
4. What might you do today to find hope in God's joy?
5. For what are you most thankful?
6. Which do you tend to be: a complainer or a praiser. Satisfied or dissatisfied? Why?

Finding Hope in God's Love – Philippians 2:1-11

For God so loved the world that he gave his one and only Son, that whoever believes in him shall not perish but have eternal life. For God did not send his Son into the world to condemn the world, but to save the world through him. John 3:16-17

To ponder our world and all of its wonder, we can't help but reflect on the majesty of God. The first chapter of Romans tells us that since the creation of the world God's invisible qualities – his eternal power and divine nature- have been clearly seen. We enjoy the morning light, the birds of the air, beautiful flowers and the warmth of family and friends. Yes, we see evil all around us, but our faith and Holy Scripture help us keep focus. God is not done, He will triumph.

Expressions of God's love are visible throughout both the Old and the New Testaments. Even in the midst of wars, disobedience, and evil, God's love demanded justice. The theme of the entire Bible is the self-revelation of the God of love. In the garden of Eden, after Adam sinned, God does not call for Adam to be put to death. Instead, He seeks to reestablish a relationship with him. God cannot allow sin to stand between Him and His creation. He personally bridged the gap by sending His son, Jesus, to pay the penalty for sin. In the New Testament, John declares, "This is how we know what love is: Jesus Christ laid down his life for us" (1 John 3:16). There are some fundamental truths about God's love:

1. God alone is the source of love. And God's love calls for a response, giving us the opportunity to find our hope in His love and reach out to Him.
2. God's love is not based on merit. God does not will that any person should perish, but He does will that everyone repent and live.
3. God loves through people—specifically followers of Christ. As believers, we act as channels for His love. We have the assurance that we have passed from death to life because we love others. Once we have received God's love as His children, He expects us to love.

The command to love others is based on how God has loved us. Since believers have been the recipients of love, they must love. Since Christ has laid down his life for us, we must be willing to lay down our lives for our brothers. Christ's love compels us to become ambassadors for Christ, with a ministry of reconciliation.

A theological definition of God's love can be helpful as we consider the importance of finding hope in God's love. Theologically, God's love may be defined as "that perfection of the divine nature by which God is eternally moved to communicate himself. It is not a mere emotional impulse, but a rational and voluntary affection, having its ground in truth and holiness and its exercise in free choice."[31]

If you consider the various parts of this definition, you notice a glimpse of what it means to find hope in God's love. We

____

31 3 Paul Enns, *The Moody Handbook of Theology* (Chicago: Moody Publishers, 2008), 196.

may find hope in God's love because God is *eternally moved to communicate himself, not a mere emotional impulse, a rational and voluntary affection, grounded in truth and holiness,* and an *exercise in free choice.*

As we think of finding hope in God's love, the second chapter of the book of Philippians comes to mind. It expresses the affirmation, example, expression, and outcome of God's love.

The Affirmation of God's Love

> Therefore if you have any encouragement from being united with Christ, if any comfort from his love, if any common sharing in the Spirit, if any tenderness and compassion, then make my joy complete by being like-minded, having the same love, being one in spirit and of one mind. Philippians 2:1–2

Twentieth-century psychoanalyst Eric Fromm said that love is the ability to respond to another person's need. Fromm was certainly not a believer, but that definition is not all that bad when you consider what God's love is—He saw our sinful condition and, in love, sent His Son, Jesus, to respond to our need. Being a follower of Christ, a believer, means that we are united with Christ and comforted by His love. As a result, we find hope in God's love.

In 1 Corinthians 13, known as the great love chapter in the Bible, we read of nine things that love does: Love suffers long, rejoices in truth, bears all things, believes all things, hopes all things, endures all things, abides now, covers a multitude of sins and casts out fear (vv. 4–7). The apostle Paul also gives us a list in Romans 8:37–39 of ten things that cannot separate us from the God's love: death, life, angels, powers, things present, things to come, height, depth, and finally, no other creature. God affirms His love for us.

The Example of God's Love

The apostle Paul continues by saying that God has not only affirmed His love for us, but He has given us an example of His love—His own Son, Jesus Christ:

> Then make my joy complete by being like-minded, having the same love, being one in spirit and of one mind. Do nothing out of selfish ambition or vain conceit. Rather, in humility value others above yourselves, not looking to your own interests but each of you to the interests of the others. (Philippians 2:2–4)

Since God loves us, we are to love one another. Since God send His Son to this earth to free us from sin, that act of humility should also be reflected in our lives.

I remember hearing a story many years ago about a missionary who was trying to explain to children who Jesus Christ was. She explained that we give gifts to express our appreciation and love to another person. On special occasions we give a gift to someone because we love them and want to express our love. The story explained that later that week a young boy gave her a gift, an unusual shell from the ocean quite some distance away. She knew that it would be a walk of several hours for the boy to find the shell, so she asked him about how he found the shell. He obviously learned the point of her Bible story because he told her that Jesus walked a long way to the cross to show his love. The boy told the missionary that the long walk to get the shell was part of the gift he was giving to her.

Warren Wiersbe concludes:

> What a paradox that a babe in a manger should be called mighty! Yet even as a baby, Jesus Christ revealed power. His birth affected the heavens as that star appeared. The star affected the Magi, and they left

their homes and made that long journey to Jerusalem. Their announcement shook King Herod and his court. Jesus' birth brought angels from heaven and simple shepherds from their flocks on the hillside. Midnight became midday as the glory of the Lord appeared to men.[32]

In 1 Corinthians 13:4-8 we read of the components of love:

"Love is patient, love is kind. It does not envy, it does not boast, it is not proud. It does not dishonor others, it is not self-seeking, it is not easily angered, it keeps no record of wrongs. Love does not delight in evil but rejoices with the truth. It always protects, always trusts, always hopes, always perseveres. Love never fails."

- Patient
- Kind
- Rejoices in the truth
- Protects
- Trusts
- Hopes
- Perseveres

Christ showed us unconditional, sacrificial love. Where would we be without His love? What kind of love do we show to one another? How can you show God's love to someone today?

The Expression of God's Love

Christ accepted the servant's place! He adopted a selfless position and entered a sinful world! The apostle Paul wrote:

In your relationships with one another, have the same mindset as Christ Jesus: Who, being in very nature God, did not consider equality with God something to be used to his own advantage; rather, he made himself

---

32 4 Warren W. Wiersbe, "His Name is Wonderful," *Christianity Today*, Vol. 30, no. 18.

> nothing by taking the very nature of a servant, being made in human likeness. And being found in appearance as a man, he humbled himself by becoming obedient to death—even death on a cross!" (Philippians 2:5–8)

In theology, we call this "the Kenosis" or "self-emptying." Jesus laid aside His glory so that He might be born in the likeness of men. He was with God the Father in eternity past, saw our sinfulness, and as an act of love, took on human flesh and left the splendors of glory. He came to this earth and allowed sinful humanity to hang him on a cross. This journey was the expression of His love for us. God declared His love, provided an example of His love, and He expressed His love.

Philip Yancey offers this insight about God's love:

"Simply reading the Bible, I encountered not a misty vapor but an actual Person. A Person as unique and distinctive and colorful as any person I know. God has deep emotions; he feels delight and frustration and anger."[33]

Followers of Christ realize that they are united with Christ and receive comfort from His love. They understand that, as believers, we have the same love as Christ and do not look out for our own interests—rather, they look out for the interests of others. Believers realize that God expressed His love through His Son Jesus who came in humility to provide salvation for us. As a result, followers of Christ follow Christ's example, and we too express humility to others.

In the same way, God loved you and me so much that He gave His signature, He gave his name, He gave His Son's body and blood. God responded to a need of sinful humanity!

---

33 Philip Yancey, *Disappointment With God* (Grand Rapids, MI: Zondervan, 1988), p 44

The outcome of God's love:

> Therefore God exalted him to the highest place and
> gave him the name that is above every name, that at
> the name of Jesus every knee should bow, in heaven
> and on earth and under the earth, and every tongue
> acknowledge that Jesus Christ is Lord, to the glory of
> God the Father. (Philippians 2:9–11)

This Christ child took on human nature. He was made in the likeness of men and found in fashion as a man. And he voluntarily assumed human nature. It was his own act, and by his own consent. He emptied himself. He divested himself of the honors and glories to clothe himself with the rags of human nature. He was in all things like to us.

God entered time and space to make a statement. He didn't come to keep us from suffering; He came to suffer as we must suffer. He didn't come to just keep us from being afraid; He came to be afraid as we are afraid. He didn't come to just keep us from dying; He came to die as we must die. He didn't come to keep us from being tempted;

He came to be tempted as we are tempted. He came to die . . . that we might life!

Imagine God's dilemma. Time and time again He tried to get His message of love through to His human creation with little response. Finally, when there was no other way, He wrapped up His message in person.

Scriptures on God's Love

> This is how God showed his love among us: He sent
> his one and only Son into the world that we might live
> through him. This is love: not that we loved God, but

that he loved us and sent his Son as an atoning sacrifice for our sins. (I John 4:9–10)

"As the Father has loved me, so have I loved you. Now remain in my love. If you keep my commands, you will remain in my love, just as I have kept my Father's commands and remain in his love. I have told you this so that my joy may be in you and that your joy may be complete. My command is this: Love each other as I have loved you. Greater love has no one than this: to lay down one's life for one's friends. This is my command: Love each other." (John 15:9-17)

In all their distress he too was distressed, and the angel of his presence saved them. In his love and mercy he redeemed them; he lifted them up and carried them all the days of old. (Isaiah 63:9)

Dear friends, let us love one another, for love comes from God. Everyone who loves has been born of God and knows God. Whoever does not love does not know God, because God is love. This is how God showed his love among us: He sent his one and only Son into the world that we might live through him. This is love: not that we loved God, but that he loved us and sent his Son as an atoning sacrifice for our sins. Dear friends, since God so loved us, we also ought to love one another. No one has ever seen God; but if we love one another, God lives in us and his love is made complete in us. (1 John 4:7-12)

Chapter 8 Discussion and Reflection Questions:
1. If you had a second life to live in unselfish service to others, what would you like to do?
2. When was the last time you shared God's love with someone?
3. When was the last time you presented the gospel to someone?
4. How can you show God's love to someone today? What will you do today to specifically show God's love?
5. When was a time you felt God's love?
6. Which of the Scriptures on God's love stands out to you most?
7. What impresses your heart and mind about the love of God today?

Finding Hope in Tragedy – Learning Lessons That Strengthen Our Faith

And we know that in all things God works for the good of those who love him, who have been called according to his purpose. Romans 8:28

We can understand that a child playing with matches will get burned. It makes sense that a reckless driver might be in a severe accident or that a chain-smoker could develop lung cancer. But it makes no sense that an innocent person would be killed seemingly for no reason at all. It is impossible for us to understand why a hurricane, tornado, tsunami, or earthquake would kill scores of innocent people. We cannot fathom why a young person, or anyone for that matter, would go on a shooting rampage and take the lives of scores of innocent people. These events defy human logic. But the Bible does have much to say about tragic events, and it is possible to find hope in tragedy.

Watch the news, and you may wonder if there is any hope left. Tragedy hits unannounced. You are never really prepared. No matter what the circumstances, sadness, heartache, and emptiness follow. Whether it comes quickly or over time, tragedy leaves you with intense pain and sorrow and raises "why questions." You may experience a flood of other (sometimes conflicting) feelings: anger, helplessness, fear, guilt, regret, loneliness, despair. When you first hear the news or experience the life-changing event, you feel like someone hit you hard right in the stomach. You try to catch your breath and be strong, but you can't. You find yourself feeling empty, stunned, overwhelmed, panicked, and very much alone.

Hope isn't optional; it's essential to our survival. You sense that you desperately need help—you are frantically grasping for hope! That is the exact moment that you need to remember that God enters through your brokenness and can give you hope in your heartache. There is hope. Please read on, my friend!

What Did I Do to Deserve This?

A good friend of mine who recently went to be with the Lord is Roy B. Zuck. He observes in *Job—Everyman's Bible Commentary*:

> Over the centuries, people have struggled with that question while agonizing in pain, crying from grief, languishing over the loss. If we could see direct relationships between our sufferings and sins in our lives—connections between our tragedies and our transgressions—we could more readily comprehend the whys of our troubles. But usually, problems intrude without explanations. And when we cannot relate our woes directly to some known acts of sin, we conclude that the afflictions are undeserved. The wail, What did I do to

deserve this? reveals a sense of injustice, a feeling that the problems exceed what we rightfully deserve.[34]

The 4,000-Year-Old Question: *Why Me?*

Why would a good God allow suffering? Over four thousand years ago, a victim of personal, family, and financial devastation asked God that penetrating question we are still asking today. In the Old Testament, Job cried to the heavens, asking:

> "I say to God: Do not declare me guilty but tell me what charges you have against me. Does it please you to oppress me, to spurn the work of your hands, while you smile on the plans of the wicked? Your hands shaped me and made me. Will you now turn and destroy me?"
> (Job 10:2–3, 8)

Job was pleading with God to tell him why He was opposing and oppressing him in such a harsh way. Job even challenged God with a series of questions in an attempt to discover why God was afflicting him. Job had experienced every loss humanly possible, and he was looking for answers as to why. Is God unjust? Job even lashed out and accused God of knowing that he was not guilty of any behavior worthy of such calamity, disaster, and misfortune. So, are there any answers? Are there any lessons found in tragedy? Here are twelve reasons why we may experience suffering and heartbreak.

1. Tragedy can come to get our attention.

In Exodus 3 and 4, we read about Moses and the burning bush. Moses was at Sinai (Mount Horeb), the very place where he would later receive the law when God called to him. Born a

---

34 Roy B. Zuck, Job—*Everyman's Bible Commentary*. Chicago, IL., Moody Publishers, 1978, p 5.

Hebrew, brought up an Egyptian, Moses faced an identity crisis, made worse by his people's rejection. As he wandered the desert, he noticed a blazing bush. He turned aside, and God met him there! In the midst of crisis, God met Moses and spoke to him—God got his attention! I remember hearing Jill Briscoe speak some years ago at a conference. She was talking about how God gets our attention, and she used an interesting phrase: "With God, any old bush will do."

Who doesn't remember the Bible story of Jonah? Whether we regard it as a Jewish folktale, "fiction with a message," or "history with a moral," there is no doubt about its central themes. If you remember Jonah's journey, you undoubtedly remember that God got Jonah's attention!

And of course, there's one of God's amazing prophets, Elijah. I've stood on Mount Carmel where the story described in 1 Kings 16–19 took place. Elijah forecast a drought and gathered all the people up to the top of Mount Carmel. He challenged them to follow God, and God gave a great victory. But following that great triumph, Elijah let fear and terror flood his heart, and he ran for his life in a panic. God got the attention of the people, and for a brief time, God got Elijah's attention.

However, God had another way to get Elijah's attention. When Elijah reached the bottom of the mountain, he found himself in depression. Elijah escaped south to the desert and Sinai (Mount Horeb), drawing fresh strength from the food and drink provided by an angel. In the place where God made himself known to Moses, he spoke to Elijah—not in any spectacular way but out of the stillness. God got Elijah's full attention.

2. Tragedy can come to remind us of alternatives and consequences.

We all make decisions, and we know that with decisions come consequences. We are not robots, and sometimes we make the wrong choice. Our primary care physician tells us to lose some

weight or to lower our salt intake. If we don't, there are consequences. We have slight chest pain and put off going to the doctor; there are consequences. Financial decisions bring implica-
tions that may be of our own doing or entirely out of our control.
How we raise our children or deal with stress and anxiety—these
and many other areas of life offer us a choice, and there are consequences. All through the Bible we read about the repercussions
of poor decision-making.

One of the best contemporary examples of a consequential
choice is misusing drugs and alcohol. We hear much today about
the opioid crisis. A 2017 New York Times article had these dire
statistics to offer:

> The current opioid epidemic is the deadliest drug cri-
> sis in American history. Overdoses, fueled by opioids,
> are the leading cause of death for Americans under
> 50 years old—killing roughly 64,000 people last year,
> more than guns or car accidents, and doing so at a pace
> faster than the H.I.V. epidemic did at its peak."[35]

I remember helping a young adult—we'll call him Jason—as
he struggled with drug addiction. He had been making bad choices, but he finally made the right decision to go to a rehab center
for six months. He thought he was "clean and sober" after rehab,
but sadly, it was not long before Jason went back to making bad
choices. He ended up back in a rehab center for six more months
. . . and then back again for a third time. Finally, he realized that
he needed to move to a different state, make all new friends, and
begin a new life, which he did.

Let's think of the alternative: a world with no choices. What
would life be without choice? Character grows and relationships

---

35 Maya Salam, "The Opiod Epidemic: A Crisis Years in the Making," *New
York Times*, October 26, 2017, https://www.nytimes.com/2017/10/26/us/
opioid-crisis-public-health-emergency.html.

deepen in the presence of real choice. There is something profound in the word *choice.* We take that word for granted. We make decisions every day. We choose to sleep in or get up early. We decide to go golf or ride a bike or exercise. We choose what we want to eat and where we want to go. Every day we face scores of choices. Then one day something happens that we did not choose. A doctor tells us that surgery is needed, and we have no choice. We're walking along on a sidewalk, trip on a raised piece of cement, fall, and must go to the hospital. That indeed was not our choice. The stock market crashes, and we lose our retirement funds. We don't choose that, but it happens.

Some choices have more significant consequences than others, like when we choose between something good or evil. We read in the book of Genesis that God gave Adam and Eve a choice. The opening chapters chronicle that they made the wrong choice and there were consequences:

> The Lord God took the man and put him in the Garden of Eden to work it and take care of it. And the Lord God commanded the man, "You are free to eat from any tree in the garden, but you must not eat from the tree of the knowledge of good and evil, for when you eat from it, you will certainly die." (Genesis 2:15–17)

It is interesting to speculate about "what if," but we know that Adam and Eve made the wrong choice, and we know that we also make wrong choices. In my first-year theology class I remember debating the question, "Do we sin because we're sinners or are we sinners because we sin?" The simple answer is that both are true. Sin entered the world because God offered a choice. The fact is that a loving and all-wise God gave our first parents a "moral option." They had a choice; we have a choice. We may follow God or reject God, accept His love or reject His love. We have the freedom of choice. We are not robots. God gave us a free will to choose.

One of the reasons that storms come into our life is because we have the freedom to choose.

3. Tragedy can come to warn us of something more serious; God sees the big picture.

That slight chest pain may upset your schedule, but if you see a cardiologist and prevent a heart attack, chances are you will be grateful for that small interruption. It was a blessing in disguise.

Perhaps you have surgery and experience a stroke in the process. You ask, "Why me?" But during those following therapy sessions, you are forced to slow down and think about life, family, and God.

The apostle Paul encourages us in 2 Corinthians 12:9–10:

> But he said to me, "My grace is sufficient for you, for my power is made perfect in weakness." Therefore I will boast all the more gladly about my weaknesses, so that Christ's power may rest on me. That is why, for Christ's sake, I delight in weaknesses, in insults, in hardships, in persecutions, in difficulties. For when I am weak, then I am strong."

Paul's words in 2 Corinthians 1:3–4 also remind us:

> Praise be to the God and Father of our Lord Jesus Christ, the Father of compassion and the God of all comfort, who comforts us in all our troubles, so that we can comfort those in any trouble with the comfort we ourselves have received from God."

4. Tragedy can come to teach us patience and grace.

Western culture has become a society of instant gratification, and we know little about patience or waiting. We click on the computer and get impatient if it does not come up immediately. We are so "in your face" and slow to offer grace to those who offend us.

The apostle Peter reminds us of our New Birth, our living hope and glorious inheritance that *transforms* us when we become a follower of Christ. Sometimes tragedy reveals what is in our innermost being. In 1 Peter 1:5-12, Peter writes that life brings trials producing the proof of our faith (v 6). People use fire to purify gold; God uses tests to distinguish between genuine and superficial faith. Faith is so much more valuable than gold. And the apostle goes on to say in verse 7 that all of this results in praise and glory to the Father. "In all this, you greatly rejoice, though now for a little while you may have had to suffer grief in all kinds of trials. These have come so that the proven genuineness of your faith—of greater worth than gold, which perishes even though refined by fire—may result in praise, glory, and honor when Jesus Christ is revealed. Though you have not seen him, you love him; and even though you do not see him now, you believe in him and are filled with an inexpressible and glorious joy" 1 Peter 1:6-8.

We can learn much about patience and grace as we go through trials. We can learn to be grateful for the memories that we have, and we can grow through the experience and become a better person rather than a bitter person.

5. Tragedy can come to remind us that each day is a gift from God.

Life is short, and each day is a gift from God. For followers of Jesus, heaven awaits and tragedy can give us a glimpse of what is beyond this life.

Most of us remember the musical Annie and the iconic song "Tomorrow." For many, life seems to have come to an end and there is no hope for tomorrow. Life events have taken them to the edge of eternity! The apostle Paul wrote in the New Testament, "I consider that our present sufferings are not worth comparing with the glory that will be revealed in us. For the creation waits in eager expectation for the children of God to be revealed" (Romans 8:18–19).

There's an old gospel song that reminds us that God hasn't promised us "skies always blue and flower-strewn pathways all our lives through," but He has promised us strength.

The apostle Peter wrote:

> In this, you greatly rejoice, though now for a little while you may have had to suffer grief in all kinds of trials. These have come so that your faith—of greater worth than gold, which perishes even though refined by fire—may be proved genuine and may result in praise, glory, and honor when Jesus Christ is revealed. Though you have not seen him, you love him; and even though you do not see him now, you believe in him and are filled with an inexpressible and glorious joy. (1 Peter 1:6–8)

6. Tragedy can come to help us grow closer to God, family, and friends.

I've made hundreds of hospital visits over the years, and one thing I have noticed is that when tragedy hits, most people call out to God, family, and close friends. I was asked to do a graveside service for a young woman who committed suicide, leaving behind two young children and a loving husband. In the midst of their profound loss and sorrow, they stood hugging and holding on to one another. They asked me if we could recite the Twenty-third Psalm together and pray the Lord's Prayer. Even during anguish and despair, their loss and tragedy brought them closer to God, family, and friends.

In James 4:8, the writer reminds us to "come near to God and He will come near to you." We hold on to things in this life until we eventually see a glimpse of eternity and begin to understand that eternal things are what have real significance.

Tragedy can help us grow closer to God, family, and friends.

7. Tragedy can come to strengthen our faith.

The book of Job is a beautiful story of one man's faithfulness to God, even when his life has fallen apart. In Job 1:21 (KJV), we read the familiar words, "The LORD gave, and the LORD hath taken away; blessed be the name of the LORD." Job faced horrific losses (12:1–13:12), asked intensely honest questions (13:13–28), and found God's profound answers (14–15). "And he said to the human race, 'The fear of the LORD—that is wisdom, and to shun evil is understanding' " (Job 28:28).

My wife and I were serving in our second congregation when she was expecting our second child. As sometimes is the case, something went wrong. The night of the miscarriage was traumatic for both of us. She began bleeding, and the bleeding just would not stop. Before I could get her to the emergency room, she had the miscarriage at home, and we were both devastated beyond words. We don't always understand why things happen as they do. In fact, things often occur that seem unexplainable. Though God may not explain, God will not abandon us. Hebrews 12:5 reminds us not to lose heart.

8. Tragedy can come to remind us of God's comfort.

> But he said to me, "My grace is sufficient for you, for my power is made perfect in weakness. Therefore, boast all the more gladly about my weaknesses, so that Christ's power may rest on me. 2 Corinthians 12:9

In late July one summer, we received an email from my wife's sister. Her daughter desperately wanted to have a baby. After many months she finally got pregnant, but sadly, the young couple found that something was wrong. The email read, "There are so many things wrong with the baby; our daughter received word today that the baby will not live. The kidneys are a lot bigger than they should be, and they are full of cysts. Oh, how they need our prayers. It's so hard seeing our kids go through this."

In early August we received this email update: "Thanks for your prayers. It continues to be a hard time for everyone. They are planning a family graveside service and are going to ask Dad to say some words. They have a little casket picked out. We are now praying that God will take this child soon. Another month is a long time to wait. The hardest part of seeing your kids go through something like this is that there's nothing to do to make it better. We thank God that we do have strong support at our church."

Some heartbreak in life cannot be restored by psychologists, counselors, medications, self-help books, or any other human resources. Some of life's trials can only be healed by God. Tragedy can come to remind us of God's comfort.

9. Tragedy can come to remind us of the importance of priorities.

I've been with many people as they approached the end of their life. Some in the hospital, some at home, some under Hospice care. But as is usually the case, those closest to us make the most significant impact.

I remember my dad slipping away into eternity. I was serving on staff in a church in Northern California. My parents were in Southern California living in retirement. I had received the news that my dad was very ill. We had visited my parent's numerous times. I knew the family doctor. I felt comfortable that when the critical moment arrived, I would have time to spend closing hours with my dad.

However, one day when I called the hospital to talk to my dad, the nurse told me that he was in a coma. I insisted that they place the telephone receiver next to his ear. They reminded me that he had not responded to anyone or anything for a day or two. When they put the telephone receiver next to his ear, and I said the words, "Dad, how are you?" I heard these words: "David, is that *you*?" Those were the last words he spoke.

My wife and I quickly drove down to visit dad in the hospital only to realize we were too late. A close friend was there with me in the hospital. He stood by my side in the hospital room, but he remained silent. Not one word was spoken, even during the long walk out of the lobby across the parking lot to the car. His arm was around me. When we reached the car, I looked at him and quietly whispered, "Thank you, my friend."

Tragedy can come to remind us of our priorities.

10. Tragedy can come to allow us to see God at work turning something around for our good.

The prophet Isaiah reminds us that God said, "For my thoughts are not your thoughts, neither are your ways my ways . . . As the heavens are higher than the earth, so are my ways higher than your ways and my thoughts than your thoughts" (Isaiah 55:8–9).

A tragedy in our life can offer us an opportunity to help someone else who may be experiencing the same heartache. A woman in our church recently told me that her adult daughter had been an alcoholic for about thirty years. This mother's hopeful prayers finally came to fruition when her daughter "hit bottom," decided to get help, and turned her life around completely. The woman who was sharing this with me said that she could see good in the years of sorrow because now her daughter wanted to help others struggling with alcoholism. The mother and daughter had a renewed emotional and spiritual relationship, and both had a sincere desire to help others who were struggling. There was hope in their tragedy.

Remember that tragedy can come to allow us to see God at work turning something around for our good.

11. Tragedy can come to stretch us emotionally and spiritually.

We've all seen signs that read, "We will rebuild" or "God isn't finished with me yet." These little statements express hope. Hope is an essential word.

Both the apostle Paul and the writer of the book of James remind us that tragedy may stretch us emotionally and spiritually:

> Consider it pure joy, my brothers, whenever you face trials of many kinds because you know that the testing of your faith develops perseverance. Perseverance must finish its work so that you may be mature and complete, not lacking anything. If any of you lacks wisdom, he should ask God, who gives generously to all without finding fault, and it will be given to him. (James 1:2–5)

> I consider that our present sufferings are not worth comparing with the glory that will be revealed in us. For the creation waits in eager expectation for the children of God to be revealed. (Romans 8:18–19)

12. Tragedy can come to show us God's plans and help us remain in His will.

Luis Palau writes, "Events never spiral out of God's control as if He somehow lacks the power or insight to direct the affairs of our little planet."[36]

---

36 Luis Palau, *Where Is God When Bad Things Happen?* (New York: Doubleday, 2000).

God is sovereign. We may begin to lose sight of that fact, but God is still there to reveal His plans for our lives and to draw us closer to Him. In the moment we may not understand. We may lash out in anger and ask WHY? But before we were born, God knew exactly how long we would live and how we would die. In Psalm 139:16 we read, "All the days ordained for me were written in your book before one of them came to be."

Oxford professor C.S. Lewis wrote years ago that pain is God's "megaphone to a deaf world."[37] Tragedy can come as a wake-up call to us. Sometimes God allows tragedy to grab us and show us His plans for our life.

Chapter 9 Discussion and Reflection Questions:
1. How do people you know deal with life's challenges?
2. How do they (or you) hear what God might be saying in the challenges?
3. What do you think a distinctively Christian viewpoint might be when it comes to life's problems, challenges, and even tragic events?
4. How do you think Job viewed his possessions? What is your view of your possessions?
5. If you were to lose everything within the next week, what would be your biggest question?
6. When was the last time your faith was seriously tested, and what was your response?
7. What do you find challenges your life the most?
   a. Financial loss
   b. Life-threatening illness
   c. Serious accident
   d. Natural disaster
   e. Death in the family
   f. War

---

37 5 C. S. Lewis, *The Problem of Pain* (New York: HarperOne, 1940, 1996).

Conclusion

In the Gospel of John, chapter 11, there is a story of HOPE. Jesus arrives and makes a powerful statement. His words are recorded in John 11:25–26: "I am the resurrection and the life. The one who believes in me will live, even though they die; and whoever lives by believing in me will never die." Jesus did not merely have the power to resurrect; His claim makes Him the very source of resurrection and a life filled with hope. That's what made His statement about a fulfilled life that is filled with hope so profound: "The thief comes only to steal and kill and destroy; I have come that they may have life and have it to the full." The Message translation puts it this way in John 10:6–10:

> Jesus told this simple story, but they had no idea what he was talking about. So he tried again. "I'll be explicit, then. I am the Gate for the sheep. All those others are up to no good—sheep stealers, every one of them. But the sheep didn't listen to them. I am the Gate. Anyone who goes through me will be cared for—will freely go in and out, and find pasture. A thief is only there to steal and kill and destroy. I came so they can have real and eternal life, more and better life than they ever dreamed of."

The Amplified Bible renders John 10:10 like this: "The thief comes only in order to steal and kill and destroy. I came that they may have and enjoy life, and have it in abundance [to the full, till it overflows].”

One of the members of Palm West Community Church has written a beautiful poem about hope and the choice that we have each hour of each day.

Our Choice Each Day

Take a look inside yourself, deep within your soul,
Are you anxious about the direction of your daily
goal?
Our world is running faster, and we feel we cannot
keep up,
So we try to satiate each moment, anxious to fill our
cup.
We are sometimes like a spray spewing out on every-
one,
We bottle up our fears inside ‘till the weight seems
like a ton.
Fear and worry choke out the flow of energy we need,
Remember when we unconsciously planted that
loathsome seed.
Today we can continue on this path that leads to noth-
ing good,
Looking back we wonder why on this road we ever
stood.
Christ is the only answer for the cares we have each
day,
We only have to ask of Him to show us the true way.
When we relinquish our own pride and put our trust
in Him,
Each moment will be brighter as we turn away from
sin.
Jesus wants to give us comfort as He knows the path

to take,
But we must surrender to His will and relinquish our
heartache.
All of us have tried to take control of our own life,
Now we wonder why we chose to partake in foolish
strife.
All the time our answer was right in front of our own
face,
Jesus was there waiting to take the burden in our
place.
Bask in the warmth of God's special plan for you,
Sweet peace and joy will come your way like the
morning dew.

Ms. Puff[38]

As you now come to the end of this book, consider three kinds of hope:

First, a living hope. "Praise be to the God and Father of our Lord Jesus Christ! In his great mercy he has given us new birth into a living hope through the resurrection of Jesus Christ from the dead" (1 Peter 1:3). We can have a living hope because of Jesus Christ. Followers of Christ have a living hope because they've committed their lives to Christ.

Second, we can have a sure hope. "We have this hope as an anchor for the soul, firm and secure. It enters the inner sanctuary behind the curtain" (Hebrews 6:19). How can we face declining health and pain? Because we have a sure hope. Hebrews 6:19 tells us this hope is an anchor, firm and secure—Jesus Christ. We can have a living hope, a sure hope.

---

38 Used with permission from Mrs Claudia Smith (Ms. Puff), active member of Palm West Community Church www.palmwestchurch.org.

Finally, we can have a blessed hope. "While we wait for the blessed hope—the appearing of the glory of our great God and Savior, Jesus Christ" (Titus 2:13).

The apostle Paul tells us that to be absent from the body is to be present with Lord.

For God so loved the world that HE GAVE.

The Holy Spirit is a source of hope, for his power causes hope to abound (Romans 15:13). Our family and friends are a source of hope. Worship offers us the opportunity to strengthen our hope. And finally, hope comes as a gift from God through grace (2 Thessalonians 2:16).

Hope leads to joy (Romans 12:12), boldness (2 Corinthians 3:12), faith, and love (Colossians 1:4-5). Hope also leads to comfort; we are to encourage one another with the knowledge of the resurrection (1 Thessalonians 4:18).

Hope has a healthy, positive impact on our life. We who look expectantly for the return of Christ, knowing that when we see Him we shall become like Him, purify ourselves "as he is pure" (1 John 3:3).

Hope also stimulates good works. Following his teaching on the resurrection of the dead, Paul exhorts his readers to do the Lord's work abundantly since such "labor is not in vain" (1 Corinthians 15:58).

Jesus suffered when He went to the cross to pay the penalty for our sin and offer us an abundant life. He is now seated at the right hand of God the Father. Until we are in heaven, God has given us the Holy Spirit to dwell within us to help us, strengthen us, and comfort us. Looking back at your experience before and during your spiritual journey with this book, think of what suffering you have gone through, but then remember the glory that is to come. Reflect on the suffering of Jesus and thank God for the glory that is ahead in heaven.

Closing Benediction

May the God of hope fill you with all joy and peace as you trust in him, so that you may overflow with hope by the power of the Holy Spirit. Romans 15:13

Appendix

Scriptures Offering Hope:

Keep your lives free from the love of money and be content with what you have, because God has said, "Never will I leave you; never will I forsake you." (Hebrews 13:5)

"Surely I am with you always, to the very end of the age." (Matthew 28:20)

"For the LORD your God is the one who goes with you to fight for you against your enemies to give you victory." (Deuteronomy 20:4)

The LORD is in his holy temple; the Lord is on his heavenly throne. He observes the sons of men; his eyes examine them. (Psalm 11:4)

You do not have because you do not ask God. (James 4:2)

You have made known to me the path of life; you will fill me with joy in your presence, with eternal pleasures at your right hand. (Psalm 16:11)

Rejoice in the LORD always. Say it again: Rejoice! Let your gentleness be evident to all. The Lord is near. (Philippians 4:4–5)

He guides the humble in what is right and teaches them his way. All the ways of the LORD are loving and faithful for those who keep the demands of his covenant. (Psalm 25:9–10)

"For I know the plans I have for you," declares the LORD, "plans to prosper you and not to harm you, plans to give you hope and a future. Then you will call upon me and come and pray to me, and listen to you. You will seek me and find me when you seek me with all your heart." (Jeremiah 29:11–13)

And we pray this in order that you may live a life worthy of the Lord and may please him in every way: bearing fruit in every good work, growing in the knowledge of God, being strengthened with all power according to his glorious might so that you may have great endurance and patience, and joyfully giving thanks to the Father, who has qualified you to share in the inheritance of the saints in the kingdom of light. (Colossians 1:10–12)

Yet I am poor and needy; may the LORD think of me. You are my help and my deliverer; O my God, do not delay. (Psalm 40:17)

How precious to me are your thoughts, O God! How vast is the sum of them! Were I to count them, they would outnumber the grains of sand. When I awake, I am still with you. (Psalm 139:17–18)

"I know that my Redeemer lives and that in the end he will stand upon the earth. And after my skin has been destroyed, yet in my flesh see God; I myself will see him with my own eyes-- I, and not another. How my heart yearns within me!" (Job 19:25–27)

Do not be anxious about anything, but in every situation, by prayer and petition, with thanksgiving, present your requests to God. And the peace of God, which transcends all understanding, will guard your hearts and your minds in Christ Jesus. Finally, brothers and sisters, whatever is true, whatever is noble, whatever is right, whatever is pure, whatever is lovely, whatever is admirable—if anything is excellent or praiseworthy—think about such things. Whatever you have learned or received or heard from me, or seen in me—put it into practice. And the God of peace will be with you. (Philippians 4:6–9)

Praise be to the God and Father of our LORD Jesus Christ! In his great mercy he has given us new birth into a living hope through the resurrection of Jesus

Christ from the dead, and into an inheritance that can never perish, spoil or fade. This inheritance is kept in heaven for you, who through faith are shielded by God's power until the coming of the salvation that is ready to be revealed in the last time. (1 Peter 1:3–5)

Be kind and compassionate to one another, forgiving each other, just as in Christ God forgave you. (Ephesians 4:32)

"Peace I leave with you; my peace I give you. I do not give to you as the world gives. Do not let your hearts be troubled and do not be afraid." (John 14:27)

"I have told you these things, so that in me you may have peace. In this world you will have trouble. But take heart! I have overcome the world." (John 16:33)

He who dwells in the shelter of the Most High will rest in the shadow of the Almighty. I will say of the Lord, "He is my refuge and my fortress, my God, in whom I trust." (Psalm 91:1–2)

Action Steps to Experience Hope:
- Accept God's forgiveness.
- Accept the fact that sometimes it is difficult to find hope and give thanks.
- Acknowledge that God IS there. God is your strength and a help to you, and He can give you hope.
- Acknowledge the power of a good friend and accept the power of God's Word, which gives us hope.
- Choose to look beyond today and remember God's precious promises of hope.
- Find a biblical support group with Christian friends to help you grow and find hope.
- Leave the impossible part up to God.
- Rejoice and say, "This IS the day that the Lord has made."
- Remember that every day is a new gift from God.
- Remember that God guides you through your life's journey.
- Remember that you are not alone, God is always there to offer you hope.

Quotes on Hope:
1. There is no medicine like hope, no incentive so great, and no tonic so powerful as expectation of something tomorrow. —Orison Swett Marden
2. Outside of the cross of Jesus Christ, there is no hope in this world. That cross and resurrection at the core of the Gospel is the only hope for humanity. Wherever you go, ask God for wisdom on how to get that Gospel in, even in the toughest situations of life. —Ravi Zacharias
3. God's mercy and grace give me hope—for myself, and for our world. —Billy Graham
4. You can make positive deposits in your own economy every day by reading and listening to powerful, positive,

life-changing content and by associating with encouraging and hope-building people. —Zig Ziglar

5. It is difficult to say what is impossible, for the dream of yesterday is the hope of today and the reality of tomorrow. —Robert H. Schuller

6. Everywhere I go I find that people... both leaders and individuals... are asking one basic question, 'Is there any hope for the future?' My answer is the same, 'Yes, through Jesus Christ.' —Billy Graham

Resources

B elow is a selected list of books, video teaching, and Christian organizations that provide hope and service opportunities for people around the world.

WEBSITES

About Depression: http://www.depression.about.com/

Anxiety Disorders Association of America: http://www.adaa.org/

Crossworld: Business as Mission (BAM) www.crossworld.org

Caregiving Children of Aging Parents: http://www.careguide.net/careguide

Christianity Online chat room with lots of information: http://forums.christianity.com/

Christianity.com: http://forums.christianity.com/

Finishers Project http://finishers.org

Global Media Outreach (GMO) www.globalmediaoutreach.com

Gospel for Asia www.winasia.org

Grace International Ministries (GIM) www.grace-international-ministries.org

Graham, Billy. *Nearing Home*. Nashville: Thomas Nelson, 2011.

Green, Brent.

Habitat for Humanity (HFHI) www.habitat.org

International School Project (ISP) www.isptrips.org

Jews for Jesus www.jewsforjesus.org

Leadership Development International (LDI) www.Idichina.com

Living Water Quilts www.LivingWaterQuilts.org

Make Today Count, 168 Panoramic, Camdenton, Missouri 65065, (314) 346-6644
Mission Aviation Fellowship (MAF) www.maf.org
National Foundation for Depressive Illness: www.depression.org
Operation Mobilisation (OM) www.om.org
Partners International www.partnersintl.org
Reach Across www.reachacross.net
SIM USA www.sim.org
St. Francis Center, 5417 Sherier Place, NW, Washington, DC 20016, 202–363–8500
Stephen Ministries: http://www.stephenministries.org/
Teach Overseas www.TeachOverseas.org
The Compassionate Friends National Headquarters, PO Box 3696, Oak Brook, IL 60522 312–990–0010
World Concern www.worldconcern.org
World Vision www.Worldvision.org
Wycliffe Bible Translators www.wycliffe.org

BOOKS

Gallagher, David P. *Healing Takes Time*. Collegeville, MN: Liturgical Press, 2005.
Haugk, Kenneth C. *When and How to use Mental Health Resources*. St. Louis, MO: Stephen Ministries, 2000.
Hollis, James. *Finding Meaning in the Second Half of Life*. New York: Gotham Books, 2005.
Johnson, Ray. *The Hope Quotient*. Nashville, TN: Thomas Nelson, 2015.
Lucado, Max. *Unshakable Hope: Building Our Lives on the Promises of God*. Nashville, TN: Thomas Nelson, 2018.
Lucado, Max. *Anxious for Nothing Finding Calm in a Chaotic World*. Study Guide ed. Nashville, TN: Thomas Nelson, 2017.
Lustbader, Wendy. *Counting on Kindness: The Dilemmas of Dependency*. New York: The Free Press, 1991.

Moore, Beth. *Whispers of Hope: 10 Weeks of Devotional Prayer.* Nashville, TN: B&H Books, 2013.

Spurgeon, Charles. *God's Promises: Of Salvation, Life, and Eternity.* Aneko Press, 2018.

Strobel, Lee. *The Case for Hope.* Grand Rapids, MI: Zondervan, 2015.

Sweeting, George. *The Joys of Successful Aging.* Chicago: Northfield Publishing, 2002.

Vaillant, George E. *Aging Well.* Little, New York: Brown and Company, 2003.

Young, David. *Celebrating the Rest of Your Life.* Minneapolis, MN: Augsburg Books, 2005.

About the Author

D r. Dave Gallagher is an adjunct professor, author, speaker and Pastor Emeritus. He teaches for Moody Distance Learning and the University of Sioux Falls. Dave holds two master's degrees (Azusa Pacific University), a doctorate (Claremont School of Theology), and is a graduate of the Moody Bible Institute (Chicago). He has five decades of pastoral ministry experience.

Dr. Gallagher is the author of three previous books: *Senior Adult Ministry in the 21st Century* (Group Publishing, 2002), *Healing Takes Time,* (Liturgical Press, 2005), and *Aging Successfully,* (Wipf & Stock, 2012). Additionally, he has contributed to eight books, written curriculum for four Christian publishers, and has had over fifty articles published.

Dr. Dave is an ordained pastor who has served in large and small churches in both urban and rural areas. In 2008 he received the Distinguished Service Award from the Moody Alumni Association. His website is www.agingsuccessfullytoday.com.

He and his wife, Mary Ann, reside in the Phoenix area. They have two adult children and two granddaughters. His hobbies are family, hiking, online teaching, preaching, reading, traveling, writing, and being with friends.

Other Books by the Author

*A**ging Successfully** offers suggestions for greater satisfaction and happiness for people over fifty. It raises spiritual and emotional issues such as how to deal with depression and gives specific action steps. This is a road map for aging. The principles come from personal experience, research, and helping people age successfully.

Loss can occur in many forms, such as the death of a loved one, divorce, or termination of a job. *Healing Takes Time* is filled with 52 meditations and reflections to help people experiencing

loss start a journey of healing. This biblical resource offers Scripture passages, personal illustrations, and practical steps to take toward healing and meditation. Just as a physical injury takes time to mend, emotional and spiritual anguish require time, patience, and faith to heal.

Senior Adult Ministry offers invaluable insights, practical ideas, and successful strategies for ministering effectively to people over 50. In this resource are 150 ministry tips, time-savers, and life-savers. It includes time tested and proven-effective ideas to help meet the social, emotional and spiritual needs of older adults. Found in most chapters, you'll find reproducible helps invaluable for sparking creativity for all areas of older adult ministry.